THE BORDER BOYS ACROSS THE FRONTIER

FREMONT B. DEERING

1st WORLD
LIBRARY
Literary Society

The Border Boys Across the Frontier

Fremont B. Deering

© 1st World Library, 2006
PO Box 2211
Fairfield, IA 52556
www.1stworldlibrary.com
First Edition

LCCN: 2006935231

Softcover ISBN: 1-4218-2484-1
Hardcover ISBN: 1-4218-2384-5
eBook ISBN: 1-4218-2584-8

Purchase *"The Border Boys Across the Frontier"*
as a traditional bound book at:
www.1stWorldLibrary.com/purchase.asp?ISBN=1-4218-2484-1

1st World Library is a literary, educational organization
dedicated to:

- Creating a free internet library of downloadable ebooks

  - Hosting writing competitions and offering book
    publishing scholarships.

Interested in more 1st World Library books?
contact: literacy@1stworldlibrary.com
Check us out at: www.1stworldlibrary.com

1ˢᵗ World Library Literary Society

Giving Back to the World

"If you want to work on the core problem, it's early school literacy."

- James Barksdale, former CEO of Netscape

"No skill is more crucial to the future of a child, or to a democratic and prosperous society, than literacy."

- Los Angeles Times

Literacy... means far more than learning how to read and write... The aim is to transmit... knowledge and promote social participation."

- UNESCO

"Literacy is not a luxury, it is a right and a responsibility. If our world is to meet the challenges of the twenty-first century we must harness the energy and creativity of all our citizens."

- President Bill Clinton

"Parents should be encouraged to read to their children, and teachers should be equipped with all available techniques for teaching literacy, so the varying needs and capacities of individual kids can be taken into account."

- Hugh Mackay

CONTENTS

CHAPTER I

THE TRAIL OF THE HAUNTED MESA

"Can you make out any sign of the mesa yet, Pete?"

The speaker, a sun-bronzed lad of about seventeen, mounted on a bright bay pony with a white-starred forehead, drew rein as he spoke. Shoving back his sombrero, he shielded his eyes from the shimmering desert glare with one hand and gazed intently off into the southwest.

"Nope; nary a speck, so fur. Queer, too; we ought to be seein' it by now."

Coyote Pete, as angular, rangy and sinewy as ever, gazed as intently in the same direction as the lad, Jack Merrill, himself. The pause allowed the remainder of the party to ride up. There was Ralph Stetson, a good deal browner and sturdier-looking than when we encountered him last in "The Border Boys on the Trail"; Walt Phelps, the ranch boy, whose blazing hair outrivaled the glowing sun; and the bony, grotesque form of Professor Wintergreen, preceptor of Latin and the kindred tongues at Stonefell College, and amateur archaeologist. Lest they might feel slighted, let us introduce also, One Spot, Two Spot and Three Spot, the pack burros.

"I always had an idea that the Haunted Mesa formed quite a prominent object in the landscape," put in Professor Wintergreen, referring to a small leather-bound book, which he had just taken from one of his saddle-bags.

"And I always had an idea," laughed Ralph Stetson, "that a landscape meant something with brooks and green trees and cows and - and things, in it."

The young son of "King Pin" Stetson, the Eastern Railroad King, looked about him at the gray desert, above which the sun blazed mercilessly down with all the intensity of a burning glass. Here and there were isolated clumps of rank-odored mesquite, the dreariest looking gray-green bush imaginable. The scanty specimens of this variety of the vegetable life of the desert were interspersed here and there by groups of scraggly, prickly cacti. Across such country as this, the party had been making its way for the past day and a half, - ever since, in fact, they had left behind them the foothills of the Hachetas, where, as we know, was located the ranch of Jack Merrill's father, and had entered the dry, almost untravelled solitudes of the Playas.

Jack Merrill consulted a compass that was strapped to his wrist.

"Well, we're keeping steadily in the right direction," he said. "Nothing for it but to keep on going; eh, Pete?"

"When yer cain't turn back, 'keep on goin's' a good word," assented the philosophical cow-puncher of the Agua Caliente, stroking his sun-bleached yellow moustache and untangling a knot in his pony's mane.

"It's up to us to get somewhere where there is water pretty quick," put in Walt Phelps; "the last time I hit the little drinking canteen I noticed that there wasn't an awful lot left in the others."

"No, and the stock's feelin' it, too," grunted Pete, digging his big, blunt-roweled spurs into his buckskin cayuse.

Followed by Jack on his Firewater, the professor on his queer, bony steed as angular as himself, Ralph on Petticoats - of exciting memory, - and Walt Phelps on his big gray, they pushed on.

The heat was blistering. In fact, to any one less accustomed to the arduous intensity of the sun's rays in this part of the country, it would have proved almost insupportable. But our party was pretty well seasoned by this time.

All of them wore the broad, leather-banded sombreros of the plainsmen except Professor Wintergreen, who had invested himself in a gigantic pith sun-helmet, from beneath which his spectacled countenance peered out, as Ralph said, "Like a toad peeking out from a mushroom." For the rest, the boys wore leather "chaps," blue shirts open at the neck, with loosely knotted red handkerchiefs about their throats. The latter were both to keep the sun off the back of their necks and to serve as protection for their mouths and nostrils against the dust in case of necessity, - as for example, when they struck a patch of burning, biting alkali. Of this pungent stuff, they had already encountered one or two stretches, and had been glad to muffle up the lower part of their faces as they rode through it.

As for Coyote Pete, those who have followed his earlier experiences are pretty familiar with that redoubtable cow-puncher's appearance; suffice it to say, therefore, that, as usual, he wore his battered leather "chaps," faded blue shirt, and his big sombrero with the silver stars affixed to the stamped leather band. In a holster he carried a rifle, as did the rest of the party, as well as his well-worn revolver. The others had provided themselves with similar weapons, although theirs glittered in blatant newness beside Pete's battered, but well-cleaned and oiled, "shootin' iron."

While they are pressing onward, with the Hachetas lying like a dim, blue cloud far behind them, let us tell the reader something about the quest that brings our party into the midst of this inhospitable place. As readers of "The Border Boys on the Trail" know, Professor Wintergreen had accompanied Jack Merrill and Ralph Stetson from Stonefell College, some weeks before, to spend a vacation on the Agua Caliente Ranch, belonging to Jack's father. The professor, as well as being on a vacation, was in a sense on a mission, for he bore with him the commission of a well-known institute of science in the East to investigate some of the mesas of this part of the world, and also to procure relics and trophies of the vanished race that once inhabited them, and accurate measurements of the strange formations.

Since their arrival at the ranch, some weeks before, events had so shaped themselves as to render the immediate undertaking of his mission impossible. The descent of Black Ramon de Barros on the ranch, as we have related, and the subsequent abduction of the boys to the old Mission across the border, had so fully occupied their attention, that all thought of the professor's errand had been lost sight of.

With Black Ramon, thanks to the boys, forever banished from his cattle-rustling raids, and the subsequent tranquility of routine life, had come a recollection of the professor's quest. Coyote Pete, a few days before this story opens, had volunteered to act as guide to the professor and his party to a mesa seldom visited except by wandering Indians and occasional cow-punchers. This was the Haunted Mesa, the location of which was so difficult to reach that previous relic-hunting expeditions had not included it in their travels.

Mr. Merrill was the more willing to allow the boys to go along, as he had been suddenly summoned into Chihuahua province, in Mexico, by reports of trouble at a mine - The Esmeralda - he owned there. Rumors of an insurrection had reached him - an insurrection which meant great peril to American interests. He had, therefore, lost no time in setting out to ascertain the true state of affairs at his mine, which, while a small one, was still likely to develop in time into an extremely valuable property.

Leaving the ranch in charge of Bud Wilson, he had started for the Mexican country without waiting for the departure of the professor's expedition. A short time later, "Professor Winter-green's Haunted Mesans," as the boys insisted on calling themselves, had likewise started on their quest. With them, at Jack Merrill's invitation, went Walter Phelps, the son of a ranching neighbor of Mr. Merrill. Walt, it will be recalled, had shared the perils and adventures of the boys across the border, as related in the previous volume, and had been the instrument of piloting them out of the mysterious valley in which Black Ramon kept his plundered herds.

Mr. Merrill's last words had been ones of caution.

"Remember, boys, that if this trouble in Mexico attains real proportions, life and property along the border may be in great danger. In such a case, it will be your immediate duty to turn back."

"But, Dad," Jack had said, "you don't expect that plundering insurrectos would have the audacity to come northward into the Playas?"

Mr. Merrill laughed.

"I didn't say there was any danger even here, my boy. Least of all, out in that barren country. If there is an insurrection, it will doubtless be put down without any trouble, but it is always well to be prepared."

Like his brother ranchers along the border, Mr. Merrill at that time had no idea of the seriousness or extent of the insurrection. Had he had, he would, of course, have prohibited the party leaving the ranch. As it was, he, in common with his neighbors, deemed the insurrection simply one of those little outbreaks that occur every now and again in Mexico, and which hitherto had been promptly squashed by Diaz's army. And so, with no real misgivings, the party had bidden the bluff, good-natured rancher good-by, little dreaming under what circumstances they were to meet again.

But all this time we have been allowing our party to travel on without bestowing any attention upon them. As the afternoon wore on, Coyote Pete began to feel real apprehension about reaching their destination that evening. Walt Phelps' fear about the water had been verified. The supply was getting low. Provided they could "pick up" the mesa they were in search of before sundown, however, this was not so serious a matter as might have been supposed. Coyote Peter knew that there was a well at the mesa, the handiwork of the ancient desert-dwellers.

The really serious thing was, that although they had apparently been traveling in the right direction, they had not yet sighted it. The cow-puncher knew, though he did not tell his young companions so, that they should long since have spied its outlines. Of the real seriousness which their position might shortly assume, the boys had as yet, little idea. Coyote Pete was not the one to alarm them unless he was convinced it was really necessary.

Suddenly, Jack, who had been riding a little in advance of the rest, gave an exclamation and pointed upward at the sun.

"Say, what's the matter with the sun?" he exclaimed.

"Sun spots, I suppose," put in Ralph Stetson jokingly.

"I see what you mean," spoke up the professor; "it has turned quite red, and there seems to be a haze overcasting the sky."

"It's getting oppressive, too," put in Walt Phelps. "What's up, Pete?"

The cow-puncher had, indeed, for some time been noticing the same phenomenon which had just attracted their notice, but he had hesitated to draw their attention to it. Now, however, he spoke, and his voice sounded grave for one of Pete's usually lively temperament.

"It means that ole Mar'm Desert is gettin' inter a tantrum," he grunted, "and that we're in an almighty fix," he added to himself.

"Is it going to rain?" inquired Ralph Stetson, as it grew rapidly darker.

"Rain?" grunted Pete. "Son, it don't rain here enough to cover the back uv a dime, even if you collect all the water that fell in a year. No, siree, what's comin' is a heap worse than rain."

"An electric storm?" queried the professor.

"No, sir - a sand storm," rejoined the cow-puncher bluntly.

CHAPTER II

THE SAND STORM

As he spoke, a queer, moaning sort of sound, something like the low, distant bellow of a steer in pain, could be heard. The air seemed filled with it. Coming from no definite direction, it yet impregnated the atmosphere. The air, too, began noticeably to thicken, until the sun, from a pallid disc - a mere ghost of its former blazing self - was blotted out altogether. A hot wind sprang up and swept witheringly about the travelers.

"Ouch!" exclaimed Ralph Stetson suddenly. "Something stung me!"

"That's the sand, son," said Coyote Pete. "The wind's commencin' ter drive it."

"Is it going to get any worse?" inquired the professor anxiously.

"A whole lot, afore it gits any better," was the disconcerting reply.

"What'll we do, Pete?" asked Jack, turning to the cow-puncher.

It had now grown so dark that he could hardly see Pete's face. It was hot, too, with a heavy, suffocating sort of heat. The wind that drove the myriads upon myriads of tiny sand grains now darkening the air, was ardent as the blast from an opened oven-door.

"Get your saddles off, quick! Lie down, and put your heads under 'em," ordered the cow-puncher, briskly swinging himself out of his saddle as he spoke.

The others hastened to follow his example. It was not a minute too soon. Already their mouths were full of gritty particles, and their eyes smarted as if they had been seared with hot irons. The ponies could hardly be induced to stand up while the process of unsaddling was gone through. As for the burros, those intelligent beasts had thrown themselves down as soon as the halt was made. With their heads laid as low as possible, and their hind quarters turned to the direction of the hot blast, they were as well prepared to weather the sand storm as they could be.

The instant the saddles were off the ponies, down they flopped, too, in the same positions as their long-eared cousins. The bipeds of the party made haste to follow their animals' example, only, in their case, their heads were sheltered as snugly as if under a tent, by the big, high-peaked, broad-flapped Mexican saddles.

It was well they had made haste, for, as Pete had said, the sand storm was evidently going to get "a whole lot worse before it got better." The air grew almost as black as night, and the wind fairly screamed as it swept over them. Jack could feel little piles of sand drifting up about them, just as driven snow forms in drifts when it strikes an obstruction. How hot it was under the saddles! The boys' mouths felt as if they would crack, so dry and feverish had they become.

"Oh, for a drink of water!" thought Jack, trying in vain to moisten his mouth by moving his tongue about within it.

All at once, above the screaming of the wind, the lad caught another sound - the galloping of hoofs coming toward them at a rapid rate. For an instant the thought flashed across him that it was their own stock that had stampeded. He stuck his head out to see, braving the furious sweep of the stinging sand.

He withdrew it like a tortoise beneath its cover, with a cry that was only half of pain. Through the driving sand he had distinctly seen three enormous forms sweep by, seen like dim shadows in the gloom around. What could they have been? In vain Jack cudgeled his brains for a solution to the mystery.

The forms he had seen drift by had been larger than any horse. So vague had their outlines been in the semi-darkness, however, that beyond an impression of their great size, he had no more definite idea of the apparitions. That they were travelling at a tremendous pace was doubtless, for hardly had he sighted them before they vanished, and he could not have had his head out of its shelter for more than a second or so.

While the lad lay in the semi-suffocation of the saddle, his mind revolved the problem, but no explanation that he could think of would fit the case. "Might they not have been wild horses?" he thought.

But no, - these were three times the size of any horse he had ever seen. Besides, their blotty-looking outlines bore no semblance to the form of a horse.

But presently something happened which put the thought of the mysterious shadows out of his mind. The wind began to abate. To be sure, at first it hardly seemed to have diminished its force, but in the course of half an hour or so the party could once more emerge, like so many ostriches, from their sand-piles, and gaze about them.

Very little sand was in the air now, but it was everywhere else. In their eyes, mouths, ears, while, if they shook their heads, a perfect little shower of it fell all about them. The animals, too, struggling to their feet out of the little mounds that had formed around them, were covered with a thick coat of grayish dust. It was a sorry-looking party. With red-rimmed eyes, cracked, parched lips and swollen tongues, they looked as if they had been dragged through a blast furnace.

The sky above them now shone with its brilliant, metallic blue once more, while ahead, the sun was sinking lower. In a short time it would have set, and, as Ralph Stetson, in a choked voice, called for "Water," the same thought flashed across the minds of all of them simultaneously.

If they didn't get water pretty soon, their predicament promised to be a serious one.

An examination of the canteens showed that not much more than a gallon remained. If only they could yet "pick up" the mesa before dark, this would not be so serious a matter, but, situated as they were, it was about as bad as bad could be.

"Waal," said Pete, at length, stroking the last grains of sand out of his bleached moustache, "waal, I reckon we might as well hang fer a sheep as er lamb, anyhow. Ef we don't hit water purty soon, we'll be thirstier yet, so we might as well fill up now."

"Illogical, but sensible," pronounced the professor, leading an eager rush for the water canteens, which were carried on the pack burros.

"Here, hold on; that's enough!" cried Jack, as Ralph Stetson bent over backward with the canteen still at his lips.

"Why, I haven't begun to drink yet," protested Ralph.

"Chaw on a bullet, son," advised Pete. "Thet's highly recommended for the thirst."

"Water suits me better," grumbled Ralph, nevertheless yielding the canteen to Jack. The lad drank sparingly, as did Pete and the others. Ralph, alone, of all the party, appeared not to realize how very precious even the little water that remained might become before long.

Refreshed even by the small quantity they had swallowed of the tepid stuff, they remounted, and Pete clambered up upon his saddle. While his pony stood motionless beneath him, he stood erect upon the leather seat. From this elevation, he scanned the horizon on every side. Far off to the southwest was sweeping a dun-colored curtain - the departing sand-storm, but that was all. Otherwise, the desert was unchanged from its previous aspect.

"Let me hev a look at thet thar compass," said Pete, resuming a sitting posture once more.

Jack extended his wrist.

"The compass is all right, I know," he said confidently.

"And I know that we've bin hitting the right trail," declared Pete. "Last time I come this way was with an old prospector who knew this part of the country well enough to 'pick up' a clump of cactus. If that compass is right, we're headed straight."

"Yes - if," put in the professor. "But are you quite sure it is?"

This was putting the matter in a new light. Not one of the party was so ignorant as not to know that, in the many miles they had traveled, the deflection of the needle, by even the smallest degree, might have meant a disastrous error.

"Why, I - I - how can it help being right?" asked Jack, a little uncertainly.

"Which side have you been carrying your revolver on?" asked the professor.

"Why, you know - on the left side," rejoined Jack, with some surprise.

Fremont B. Deering

"And the compass on the left wrist?"

"Yes. Why? Isn't it -"

"No, it ain't!" roared Pete. "I see it all now, perfusser; that thar shootin' iron has bin deflectin' ther needle."

"I fear so," rejoined the professor.

Under his direction, Jack moved the compass into various positions, and at the end of a quarter of an hour they arrived at the startling conclusion that they had travelled perhaps many miles out of their way. The metal of the weapons Jack carried having, as they saw only too clearly now, deflected the needle.

"What an idiot I was not to think of such a possibility!" exclaimed Jack bitterly.

"Not at all, my boy," comforted the professor. "The same thing has happened to experienced sea-captains, and they have navigated many miles off their course before they discovered their error."

"All of which, not bein' at' sea, don't help us any," grunted Pete. "Suppose now, perfusser, that you jes' figger out as well as you kin, how far wrong we hev gone."

"It will be a difficult task, I fear," said the professor.

"It'll be a heap difficulter task, ef we don't hit water purty soon," retorted the cow-puncher.

Thus admonished, Professor Wintergreen divested himself of his weapons, and, taking out a small notebook, began, with the compass before him, to make some calculations. At the end of ten minutes or so, he raised his head.

"Well?" asked Jack eagerly.

"Well," rejoined the professor, "it's not as bad as it might be. We are, according to my reckoning, about twenty-five miles farther to the south than we should be."

He consulted his notebook once more.

"The bearings of the mesa require us to travel in that direction." He indicated a point to the northward of where they were halted.

"And it's twenty-five miles, you say?" asked Pete.

"About that. It may be more, and again it may be less."

"Waal, the less it is, ther better it'll suit yours truly. This stock is jes' about tuckered."

With the professor now bearing the compass, they set out once more, this time taking the direction indicated by the man of science.

"Suppose the professor is wrong?" Ralph whispered to Jack, as they urged their almost exhausted cayuses onward.

Jack shrugged his shoulders.

"What's the use of supposing?" he said.

It was sun-down, and a welcome coolness had begun to be noticeable in the air, when Jack gave a shout and pointed directly ahead of them.

"Look, look!" he cried. "What's that?"

"That" was only a small purplish speck on the far horizon, but it broke the monotony of the sky-line sharply. Coyote Pete scrutinized it with keen eyes for a moment, narrowing his optics till they were mere slits. Then -

Fremont B. Deering

"Give me the glasses, perfusser," he requested. Every one in the party knew that their lives, or deaths probably, hung on the verdict of the next few seconds, but Pete's slow drawl was more pronounced and unperturbed than ever. He put the glasses to his eyes as unconcernedly as if he were searching for a bunch of estrays. Presently he lowered them.

"Is - is it -?" began Jack, while the others all bent forward in their saddles, hanging on the rejoinder.

"It is," declared Pete, and he might have said more, but the rest of his words were drowned in a ringing cheer.

CHAPTER III

A NIGHT ALARM

"How far distant do you imagine it is?" inquired the professor, as they rode forward with their drooping spirits considerably revived.

"Not more than fifteen miles - if it is that, 'cording ter my calcerlations," decided Pete.

"Then we should arrive there by ten o'clock to-night."

"About that time - yep. That is, if none of ther stock give out beforehand."

"Why do they call it the Haunted Mesa?" inquired Jack.

"Some fool old Injun notion 'bout ghosts er spirits hauntin' it," rejoined Pete.

"Just as well for us they have that idea," said Walt. "They'll give it a wide berth."

It flashed across Jack's mind at that moment to tell about the vague, gigantic shapes he had seen flit by in the gloom of the sand-storm. But, viewed in the present light, it seemed so absurd that the boy hesitated to do so.

"Maybe I was mistaken after all," he thought to himself.

22   Fremont B. Deering

"There was so much sand blowing at the time that I might very well have had a blurred vision."

The next minute he was doubly glad that he had refrained from telling of his weird experience, for the professor, in a scornful voice, spoke up.

"Such foolish superstitions did exist in the ancient days, when every bush held a spirit and every rock was supposed to be endowed with sentient life. Happily, nowadays, none but the very ignorant credit such things. By educated people they are laughed at."

Pete, who was jogging steadily on ahead of the rest of them, made no rejoinder. Ralph, however, spoke up.

"What would you do, if you were to see a spirit, professor?" he inquired, with an expression of great innocence in his round, plump face.

"I'd take after it with a good thick stick," was the ready reply. "That is, always supposing that one *could* see such a thing."

Darkness fell rapidly. Night, in fact, rushed down on them as soon almost as the sun sank behind the western rim of the desert. To the south some jagged sierras grew purple and then black in the fading light. Fortunately there was a moon, though the luminary of night was in her last quarter. However, the silvery light added to the brilliance of the desert stars, gave them all the radiance they needed to pursue their way.

The travelers could now perceive the outlines of the Haunted Mesa more clearly. It reared itself strangely out of the surrounding solitudes, almost as if it were the work of human hands, instead of the result of long-spent geological forces.

"Wish we were there now," breathed Ralph, patting his pony's sweating forequarters, "poor old Petticoats is about 'all in.'"

"It's purty hard to kill a cayuse," rejoined Pete. "I've seen 'em flourish on cottonwood leaves and alkali water - yep, and git fat on it, too. Be like a cayuse, my son, and adapt yourself to carcumstances."

"Very good advice," said the professor approvingly, as the desert philosopher concluded.

As Pete had conjectured, the ponies were far from being as tuckered out as they appeared, despite their sunken flanks and distended nostrils. As the cool night drew on, and they approached more nearly to the upraised form of the mesa, the little animals even began to prick their ears and whinny softly. The pack animals, too, seemed to pluck up spirits amazingly.

"They smell grass and water," commented Pete, as he observed these signs.

Shortly after ten, as had been surmised, they were among the bunch-grass surrounding the mesa. Striking such a spot after their long wanderings on the hot desert, was delightful, indeed. Presently, too, came to their ears the tinkling sound of flowing water.

"It's the overflow from them old-timers' well at the base of the mesa," pronounced Pete, listening.

"Yes, and here it is," cried Jack, who had been riding a short distance in advance, and had suddenly come across a small stream.

The water was but a tiny thread, but it looked as welcome just then as a whole lake. Cautioning the boys to keep their ponies back, Pete took a long-handled shovel from one of the packs, and soon excavated quite a little basin. While he had been doing this, the boys had had to restrain their thirst, for the ponies were almost crazy with impatience to get at the water. It required all the boys' management, in fact, to keep them from breaking away and getting at the water. In the heated condition of the little animals, this might have meant a case of foundering. At last Pete let the thirsty creatures take a little water, and afterward they were tethered to a clump of brush, while the boys themselves assuaged their pangs. After their first ravenous thirst was quenched - which was not soon - they took turns in dashing water over each other's heads, removing the last traces of the sand-storm. This done, they all declared that they felt like new men, - or boys, - and a unanimous cry for supper arose.

"Let me see, now," mused Pete, gazing up at the purplish, black heights of the mesa above them, "as I recollect it, there's only one path up thar. The good book says, foller the strait and narrer path, but it don't say nothing about doing it in the dark, so I reckon that the best thing we can do will be to camp right under that bluff thar, whar the water comes out, till it gets to be daylight."

This was agreed to be an excellent plan, and, accordingly, the stock having been tethered out amidst the bunch-grass, the packs were unloaded, and the work of getting a camp in shape proceeded apace. In that part of New Mexico, although it is warm enough by day, nightfall brings with it a sharp chill. It was decided, therefore, to rig up the tents and sleep under their protection. The three canvas shelters of the bell type were soon erected, and then, with mesquite roots, Coyote Pete kindled a fire and put the kettle on. Supper consisted of corned beef, canned corn and canned tomatoes, with coffee, hard biscuit and cheese.

"I'll bet we're the first folks that have eaten a meal here for many a long day," said Jack, looking about him, after his hunger had been satisfied.

"It is, in all probability, fifteen hundred years or more since the first inhabitants of this mesa dwelt here," announced the professor.

"My! My! You could boil an egg in that time," commented

Pete, drawing out his old black briar and lighting it. He lay on one elbow and began to smoke contemplatively.

The others did not speak for a few moments, so engrossed were they with the ideas that the professor had summoned up. Once, perhaps, this dead, black, empty mesa above them had held busy, bustling life. Now it stood silently brooding amid the desolation stretched about it, as solitary as the Sphinx itself.

The spot at which they were camped was the sheer, or cliff side of the mesa. At the other side they knew, from Coyote Pete's description, were numerous openings and a zig-zag pathway leading up to the very summit. It was on this summit, which according to the most accurate information obtainable had once been used for the sacrificial rites of sun worship, that the professor expected to find the relics for which he was searching.

For an hour or two the lads discussed the dead-and-gone mesa dwellers, with an occasional word from the professor, who was deeply read on the subject. This was all so much Greek to Pete, who solemnly smoked away, every now and then putting in a word or two, but for the most part lying in silence, looking out beyond the black shadow of the mesa across the moonlit desert toward the rocky hills to the south.

Suddenly, the lanky cowboy leaped to his feet with a yell that punctured the silence like a pistol-shot. In two flying leaps, he had bounded clear over the professor's head, and was in among the tents, searching for his pistol. Before one of the amazed group about the fire could collect his senses at the sudden galvanizing of Coyote Pete, he was back among them again.

"Wow!" he yelled into the night, "come on, there, you, whoever you are! Come on, I say! I'll give you a fight! Yep, big as you are, I ain't skeered of you."

"Pete! Pete! Whatever is the matter?" gasped Jack, who, with the others, was by this time on his feet.

"Matter?" howled Pete. "Matter enough. I do begin to think this place shore is haunted, or suthin'. As I lay there, I felt suthin' tiptoeing about behind me, and when I whipped suddenly round ter see if one of the critters hadn't broken loose, what did I see but a great, big, enormous thing, as big as a house, looking down at me. Afore I could say a word, it was gone."

"Gone!" echoed the others. "What was it?"

"Wish you'd tell me," sputtered the cow-puncher, looking about him, and still gripping his gun, "I never saw the like in all my born days."

"Well, what did it look like?"

"Hard to tell you," rejoined Pete. "It was as big as that." He pointed right up at the moon.

"As tall as the moon? Oh, come, Pete, you had dropped off and were dreaming," laughed Ralph.

"Who said it was as tall as the moon?" demanded the excited cow-puncher angrily. "I only meant to convey to your benighted senses some idee uv what it luked like."

"Well, how high was it?" asked Jack, in whose tones was a curious note of interest, for a reason we can guess.

"About twenty feet, as near's I could judge. It had red eyes, that glared like the tail-lamps of a train, and it spat fire, and it -"

"Whoa! Whoa!" laughed Walt Phelps. "Now we know it was a nightmare, Pete. The dream of a rarebit fiend. You ate too much crackers and cheese at supper."

"How was it we didn't see it?" asked Ralph, who had not spoken up till now.

"Why, you were lying with your back toward the direction it came from," explained Pete.

"An interesting optical delusion," declared the professor. "I must make a note of it, and -"

"Wow! There it goes ag'in."

"Where? Where?" chorused the boys.

"Right off there! Look! Look!"

The lanky cow-puncher, fairly dancing about with excitement, pointed out beyond the shadow of the solitary mesa. Sure enough, there were three or four enormous, black, shadowy shapes, traveling across the sands at a seemingly great speed.

"Get your rifles, boys!" yelled Jack.

The weapons lay handy, and in a jiffy four beads had been drawn on the immense, vague shapes.

But even as their fingers pressed the triggers, and the four reports rang out as one, the indefinite forms vanished as mysteriously as they had appeared.

CHAPTER IV

SOME QUEER TRACKS

The hour, the surroundings, and the utter mystery of the whole affair combined to make the sudden appearance and vanishment of the great shadowy shapes the more inexplicable, not to say alarming. Small wonder was it that the inquiring faces that turned toward each other were a trifle whiter than usual.

"What do you make of it, Pete?" asked Jack.

"Stumped, by the big horn spoon!" was the expressive response.

"No doubt, some natural phenomena, with a simple explanation," came from the professor. It was noted, though, that his angular form seemed to be somewhat shivery as he spoke, and that his teeth chattered like dice rattling in a box.

"Natural phe-nothings!" burst out Pete. "The things, whatever they was, were as solid as you or me."

"How was it they didn't make any noise, then?" inquired Ralph, practically.

"Waal, son, you jes' take a run on the bunchgrass, and you'll see that you won't make no racket, nuther."

Ralph did as he was directed, and it was really wonderful how silently he sped over the springy vegetation.

"Maybe it was somebody putting up a scare on us," suggested Walt, rather lamely.

"They couldn't rig up anything as big as that," said Jack decisively, "besides, there's another thing - I didn't tell you because I thought I might have been mistaken, but I saw those same things this afternoon."

"What?" went up in a perfect roar of incredulity.

"Say, is this some kind of a josh?" asked Coyote Pete suspiciously.

"Never more serious in my life," Jack assured him, and then went on to relate the strange experience that had befallen him when he had poked his head out from under the saddle in the sand-storm.

"If they weren't so enormous, I should say they was horses," said Pete; "but the biggest horses that ever growed never even approached them critters - spooks, er whatever they are."

"There are giants among men," suggested Walt, "why shouldn't there be giants among spooks, too?"

"You get to Halifax with that spook talk," said Coyote Pete scornfully. "I'll bet my Sunday sombrero that whatever them things is, there's some sore of human mischief back uv it. But what is it? Who put it up?"

"Yes, and what for, and why?" laughed Jack. "I tell you, fellows," he went on, "it's no use of our racking our brains to-night over this. The best thing we can do is to set a watch. Then, if they come again, we can try a shot at them. If not, why then in the morning we'll make an investigation; eh?"

"Durn good advice," grunted Coyote Pete. "Now, I'd suggest that ther perfusser takes ther fust watch, and -"

"No, no, my dear sir; really, I - I have a cold already. A-hem - ach-oo!"

The man of science, it seemed, had really developed serious bronchial trouble in record time.

"Why, professor," said Jack mischievously, "haven't I heard you say that you'd like a chance to investigate such a phenomenon as this?"

"Hum, yes - yes, my young friend. I may have said so, yes. And any other time I should be only too pleased to - Good Land! what's that?"

With the agility of a grasshopper, the professor had jumped fully three feet, as one of the pack-burros, nosing about behind him, accidentally butted him in the small of his back. The others burst into a roar of laughter, which they could not check. The professor, however, adjusted his spectacles solemnly and looked about him with much dignity.

"I thought I saw a book I had dropped, almost in the fire," he explained glibly, "so I jumped to get it before a hot ember fell on it."

"I had no idea you could jump like that, professor," laughed Jack. "You should have gone in for athletics at Stonefell."

It was finally decided that Walt and Ralph should stand the first watch, and Coyote Pete and Jack the last part of the night. The professor, after carefully drawing tight the curtain of his tent, "to keep the cold out," as he explained, retired. Soon after, Jack and the cow-puncher also went to bed till the watch should summon them to go on duty in their turn.

But the night passed without any reappearance of the strange shapes which had so upset the tranquility of the little camp, and, viewed in the fresh light of a new and glorious day, somehow the affair did not seem nearly so ominous and awe-inspiring as it had the night before. Breakfast, as you may imagine, was speedily disposed of, and, having seen to the stock, the party started out to explore the mesa itself.

As has been said, the side upon which they had camped the night before was nothing but a sheer cliff. Under the guidance of Coyote Pete, they now set out to encircle the strange precipitous formation. Their hearts beat high, and their eyes shone with an aroused sense of adventure as they strode along.

The professor carried with him a small volume containing a partial translation of the symbols and sign language of the ancient tribe whose domains they were about to invade. Jack had a coil of stout, half-inch manila rope, about two hundred feet in length. Walt Phelps' burden was a shovel, while Ralph Stetson carried an axe. All bore with them their revolvers, and Coyote Pete carried, in addition, a rifle.

"Are you afraid of anything?" the professor had asked him, as he noticed the sun-bronzed plainsman pick up this latter weapon.

"Waal," Pete had rejoined, with a portentous wink at the boys, "you never kin tell in this wale of tears what you're a-goin' up aginst - queer shapes, fer instance."

As they strode along, naturally the subject of the shadowy forms which had alarmed them the night before arose. Jack would have liked to investigate them right then and there, but, after all, he decided with the rest of the party, that an exploration of the mesa was the first thing of importance to be accomplished. And an interesting sight the great abandoned aboriginal beehive, was, as they rounded the inaccessible side and emerged upon the portion which faced toward the northwest.

Pete's recollection had not played him false. There was a rough pathway constructed up its face upon this side, and at the top were three tiers of holes bored in the rock face. These were evidently intended for windows, as a larger aperture was just as evidently meant for a door. The path, which zig-zagged up the face of the mesa was about eight inches in width, not more, at its base, and varied - so far as they could see from below - from that breadth to a foot, as it grew higher.

From the base to the summit the mesa was probably about one hundred and fifty feet in height, the windows not commencing till within twenty feet of the top. Its length at the base was, roughly, three hundred feet, and its thickness varied from three hundred feet or more at the center, to a few feet at each end. Roughly, then, its basic outline was that of an irregular parallelogram, while its profile was that of a flat-topped cone. For some moments the little group stood in silence as they gazed up at the yellowish-gray walls of the once-active mound.

Finally, recovering from their reverie, they set out after Coyote Pete to scale the narrow pathway leading to the summit. But, as the cow-puncher set his feet on the lowermost part of the path, he gave an exclamation of astonishment and pointed downward.

There in the dust was a footprint, - several of them, in fact.

It was a startling discovery in that isolated part of the desert to come upon the traces of human occupancy. Robinson Crusoe on his desert island could not have looked any more astonished at the imprint of the savage's sole, than did Coyote Pete. He stood looking down speechlessly at his discovery, while the others crowded about him, asking a dozen questions at once.

"If the sand-storm had hit this section, we'd been able to form some idee of how long ago them hoofs was planted there," said Pete; "but as it is, ther feller who wondered how ther apple got in ther dumpling didn't hev a harder problem than the nut we've got to crack."

"There must have been several of them," said Jack, who had been gazing in the dust, which lay thick on the pathway to the summit of the mesa.

"A dozen at least," nodded Pete. He tipped back his sombrero and scratched his ruffled hair, fairly at a standstill to account for what they had encountered.

"Mightn't it have been prospectors?" asked Ralph.

"Might hev bin, yes," agreed Pete; "but, fer one thing, my son, prospectors don't usually travel in dozens."

"Hum - that's so," assented Jack, who at first had greeted Ralph's suggestion eagerly.

"Look here!" cried Ralph suddenly, holding up a glittering object which he had just discerned in the bunch-grass at the base of the mesa.

"What is it, my boy?" inquired the professor.

Ralph extended the object for their inspection.

"A strange coin," cried Walt.

"Not so blamed strange, either," said Pete, picking it off the boy's palm and examining it. "It's a Mexican peso."

"Then the men who were here were Mexicans?" cried Jack.

"Not so fast, my boy," admonished Pete. "Might as well say that every feller who finds a Canadian dime in his pocket is a Kanuck. Say," he suggested suddenly, "suppose you boys jes' see if you can find any tracks around the base of the mesa."

They scattered and looked carefully about them, but the bunch-grass grew in quite a broad belt all about, and no footmarks could be discerned. Nor did a careful examination of the grass show any broken or trampled blades, as would have been the case had ponies been there recently.

"That decides it," announced Pete, after this last fact had been ascertained, "whoever made those foot-marks wasn't here recent, that's a fact. But who could they have been, and what brought them here?"

"Maybe Indians," suggested Ralph sagely.

"Yep, if Indians wore boots, which they don't," grinned Pete, while poor Ralph colored to the roots of his hair over the general laugh that arose at his expense.

"I think," announced the professor finally, "that it would be our best plan to go ahead exploring the mesa. After all, there is nothing here that can hurt us. Those ruffians of Black Ramon's have been driven out of the country, and, anyway, they would not be likely to come here. As for Indians, their reservation is many miles to the north-east. Whoever was here, was either on a scientific quest, like ourselves, or else unfortunately lost in the desert."

"Jes' ther same," grunted Pete, in a low voice that nobody overheard, "I'd like ter know what all this means: Big, shadowy shapes flitting around in ther night, and footsteps here in ther mornin'. It don't look right."

He took a swift glance all about him. In every direction lay the desert - glittering, far-reaching, lonely as the open sea. The only break in the monotony came to the south - on the border - where stretched the rocky, desolate ridge.

"No one wouldn't come here without an object," reasoned Pete to himself, as they began the ascent of the narrow, tortuous trail, "now, what in thunder could that objec' hev bin?"

CHAPTER V

THE HOLLOW ALTAR

"Magnificent indeed!"

The words, falling from the professor's lips, echoed hollowly against the walls of the lofty, vaulted chamber in which the adventurers found themselves, after traversing a narrow passage leading inward from the causeway.

The walls of this chamber, which must have been fully thirty feet in height at its greatest altitude, were formed of the soft rock, out of which it had been excavated apparently uncounted ages before. They were daubed with grotesque figures in faded, but still discernible, colors. Most of these figures had to do with scenes of violence, and in almost all of them the figure of what appeared to be an enormous rattlesnake, with human head and arms, predominated.

Among the mural decorations were some that puzzled the professor considerably. They were crude drawings of men in what appeared to be intended for boats. The professor found these inexplicable. The very idea of boats in that arid spot seemed absurdly out of place. Why, then, should the mesa-dwellers have depicted them?

Light was furnished to the chamber by an irregularly shaped hole in the roof above. Although there was plenty of illumination, it had yet been some moments before the adventurers, coming out of the brilliant sunlight outside, grew used enough to the gloom to make out their surroundings. When they did so, the first words uttered were those of the professor recorded above.

Like some queer, long-legged bird, the man of science, with a giant magnifying glass held up to his eye, sped hither and thither on his long, angular limbs, inspecting minutely the drawings and crude attempts at decoration. Already he had out his tape-measure and sketch-book, making observations and recording measurements. Presently, however, he recalled himself from the first heat of his enthusiasm.

"After all," he said, "we shall have plenty of time in which to explore this chamber, which seems to have been used as a council hall. Let us examine the remainder of this remarkable place."

"You may well call it that, perfusser," grunted Pete. "It's remarkable fer the dust thet's in it, if nothing else. But what I'd like to know," he added to himself, "is jes' whar the owners of them footsteps vanished themselves to."

Which brings us to a remarkable discovery, made a few moments before our party had entered the "Council Hall," as the professor called it.

As you may imagine, they had traced the footsteps with some care, hoping to come upon a solution of the mystery of their origin. Picture their astonishment, then, when you are told that the footsteps abruptly vanished at the summit of the zig-zag trail. Although dust lay thick on the chambers within the mesa, not a solitary foot-mark marred its soft gray surface. With the exception of the numerous footsteps on the trail to the summit, there was no other sign of human visitors.

Like most old plainsmen and all wild animals, Pete was suspicious of anything he couldn't understand, and it certainly did seem inexplicable that a party of men should have visited the mesa and contented themselves with running or walking up and down the causeway outside, or promenading the summit. Such, however, appeared to be the only explanation, and as such they were forced to accept it.

But such speculations as these were far from monopolizing the minds of the professor and the boys. They eagerly traversed chamber after chamber, finding these latter to be small "apartments," so to speak, giving upon a common passage just beyond the "Council Hall." The professor told them that each of these small chambers was formerly the home of an aboriginal family. In the floor of the passage he pointed to numerous bowl-like holes, which, according to him, had been used for the sharpening of spears and arrow heads.

In some of the small chambers specimens of rude pottery were found, all ornamented with the same figure of the human-headed rattlesnake. Evidently the form represented must have been a deity of the tribe. Each of the small chambers was lighted by one of the holes cut in the face of the cliff, which they had noticed from below. The boys darted in and out of the various rock chambers, like ferrets in a rabbit warren, followed at a more leisurely pace by the professor and Coyote Pete.

"Maybe we'll find some treasure," suggested Ralph Stetson, as, with flushed faces, plentifully begrimed with dust, they paused in the last of the rocky chambers.

"Say, you've got treasure on the brain, ever since we found that chest of Jim Hicks' in the passage-way under the old mission, and started our bank accounts," laughed Jack. "You must be forgetting that this mesa has been visited frequently by cattlemen and wandering prospectors."

"Well, I should hardly call it frequently, Jack," put in Professor Wintergreen, who was now standing with Coyote Pete at his elbow, in the narrow entrance to the rocky chamber.

"Nope," added Coyote Pete; "you can bet your boots we didn't come here except when we had to. In the past, though, it made a mighty good watering-place for the cattlemen driving from one section of this country to another. Sence they cut up that land over to the westward inter farms, though, the big cattle drives have stopped, and I don't suppose any one's bin around here for a long time, 'cepting those varmints whose feet-marks we seen."

"How do you know they are varmints?" laughed Walt Phelps.

"Don't see what business they'd hev here otherwise, and -" began Pete, but a perfect tempest of laughter at his expense drowned the rest of his speech.

"Well, now that we seem to have pretty well explored the habitation part of the mesa, let us make our way to the summit," suggested the professor.

With a whoop and yell, the excited boys followed the suggestion at once, and a dash up the narrow causeway followed at imminent risk of one of another losing his footing.

"Hey, hold on thar!" yelled Pete, as they dashed upward, "we don't want no funerals here, an' it's er drop of more'n a hundred feet to ther ground."

This rather checked the boys' enthusiasm, and they went more slowly thereafter.

The summit of the mesa was found to consist of a small plateau, about a quarter of an acre in extent, perfectly bare, and shaped like a saucer. Near the center was the hole which gave illumination to the council hall below them, while in a spot almost exactly in the middle of the queer elevation, was a rough, square erection of sun-baked brick. This was about twelve feet in length, five feet in height, and six feet or so through. Apparently it had once been a kind of an altar. The professor thought this assumption tenable, as it was known that the aborigines who had once inhabited the mesa had been sun-worshipers.

"Ugh!" shuddered Jack, as he gazed at the altar. "And they used to offer human sacrifices here."

"I think it altogether likely," said the professor calmly; "probably that altar has witnessed the immolation of more than a hundred victims at a single tribal ceremony."

Ralph Stetson was clambering up on the altar as the professor spoke, but at hearing these words he hastily descended again.

"I guess I'll defer examining it till some other time," he said decidedly.

From the summit of the mesa a wonderful view could be obtained. At that altitude the rocky, desolate range of sierras to the south could be seen clearly, although a mile or so distant.

"Thar's the border yonder," said Pete, pointing.

"And over across there is father, I guess," said Jack. "I hope he found everything at the Esmeralda all right."

"Sure he did," said Pete confidently. "I tell you, these greaser uprisings don't amount to a busted gourd. Mister Diaz's tin soldiers come along, and 'pop-bang! Adios!' It's all over."

"But I have heard that in this case the insurrectionists of Northern Chihuahua are exceptionally well provided with arms and ammunition," objected the professor. "The American government can't make out from whence they are supplied with guns and munitions of war."

"Huh, where'd they git 'em from, I'd like to know?" snorted Pete. "The border is well guarded at any point where they would be likely to ship 'em across, and -"

"How about the *unlikely* points?" inquired the professor amiably.

"Um - ah - well," began Pete, somewhat stumped by this last, "I don't see what that's got to do with it."

"But I do. Mexicans, my friend, are, as you should know, a cunning race. Moreover, those of them who dwell along it know the border far better than any white could ever hope to. By the admission of our own secret agents, it has hitherto been impossible to find how the arms, which the Chihuahua rebels are receiving, can reach them. It is obvious, however, that there must be some way in which they do, hence -"

"Waal, perfusser, hev it your own way," grunted Pete, rather red and angry. The professor's logic did indeed seem unassailable. The rebels of Northern Chihuahua were getting arms - but how? The cow-puncher and the boys recalled now a visit made to Mr. Merrill's ranch some weeks before by a party of United States secret agents.

The men were puzzled and angry over their failure to locate the "leak." Somehow arms were being shipped across the border into Chihuahua from American soil, but just how had hitherto baffled all the efforts of their ingenuity to discover.

"There, there, don't be so easily offended," counseled the professor, perceiving Pete's palpable irritation. "After all, the matter has nothing to do with us. We are here to measure the mesa for scientific purposes, not to get into arguments over how a band of insurrectos are getting their arms. Come, boys, to work. Let us begin at the top, by measuring the altar. Suppose, Jack, you lay the tape on it, while I make a rough field sketch of the structure."

The boys, now over their first repulsion to having anything to do with the altar, about which such grisly memories clustered, eagerly began to carry out these orders, while Coyote Pete seated himself on the side of the summit overlooking the travelers' camp below, and amused himself by throwing small bits of detached rock down at the unoffending One Spot, Two Spot and Three Spot.

The base of the altar being duly measured and recorded, Jack, tape in hand, followed by the others, clambered up its rough sides, which afforded an easy foothold, for the purpose of ascertaining the dimensions of the top. To the lad's astonishment, however, there was no summit. That is to say, the altar was hollow.

The professor exhibited considerable scientific excitement on hearing this. The man of science had been greatly puzzled over the total absence of any traces of the human sacrifices he knew must have taken place there. He now hailed Jack eagerly.

"Are there not some bones or traces of sacrifices inside it, my boy?" he inquired excitedly.

"Nary a bone," shouted Walter cheerfully.

"Hold on, though," cried Jack. "There are some queer-looking things down in one corner."

Lowering himself inside the altar, he made for one corner of the erection, in which he had spied a heap of fragile-looking bones of some kind.

"Skeletons of snakes!" he cried, holding up one of these for the inspection of the professor, who had by this time hoisted his bony frame over the top of the altar and now stood beside them.

"That's right, my boy; they are serpents' skeletons. Doubtless in their sacrificial ceremonies these people also offered up rattlesnakes, which seem to have been a sort of sacred reptile among them; much as, in a sense, the cat was sacred to the ancient Egyptians, and the python is worshiped in certain parts of India."

"But, professor," protested Jack, "if, as you say, numerous human sacrifices were offered here in the past, why do we not find any human remains here?"

"Who can say, my boy? Many of the habits of these pre-historic peoples are veiled in mystery. We can only surmise and reconstruct. They may have burned them or disposed of them in some other way."

"Say!" exclaimed Ralph suddenly. "This floor sounds to me as if it was hollow; maybe there's a chamber or something underneath."

The boy, who had been stamping about with a vague sense of making some such discovery, hailed them with excited looks.

"Hollow, you say?" asked the professor, with every appearance of deep interest.

"Yes, listen!"

Again Ralph stamped about. There was no question about it - the stone-paving, of which the floor of the altar was formed, gave out an unmistakably hollow sound.

The professor was down on his hands and knees instantly, searching about, like a hound on the scent. In the meantime the others stamped about in other parts of the interior, but only where Ralph's feet had given out the hollow sound did the floor appear anything but solid.

"Queer!" exclaimed the professor, as, after a considerable search, he rose to his feet covered with dust and streaming with perspiration, "there should be some sort of trap-door here, to judge by the sounds, but so far as I can see, the joints between the pavement are perfectly tight, and I can find no ring or lever which might open such an aperture."

"Perhaps -" began Ralph, but he was interrupted by a sudden

wild yell from Pete.

"Wow! Yee-ow! Come here quick, everybody!"

Fremont B. Deering

CHAPTER VI

THE LEGEND OF A FORGOTTEN RACE

Leaping and scrambling over the top of the hollow altar to the best of their abilities, the four explorers found their cow-puncher friend dancing wildly about on the edge of the mesa, in imminent peril of tumbling over altogether. He was wildly excited, and, as they emerged, he pointed down over the cliff edge.

"Whatever is the matter?" exclaimed Jack, regarding the antics of the usually staid cow-puncher with amazement.

"The stock! Look at the stock!" yelled Pete.

Peering over the edge at the bunch-grass belt in which their ponies were tethered, the adventurers saw a spectacle which might well have been calculated to excite the cow-puncher. One Spot, Two Spot and Three Spot were tearing round and round at the end of their tethers, in the wildest alarm, evidently, while the cayuses were stamping and snorting, with distended nostrils and wild, frightened eyes.

"What's the matter with them?" gasped Walt, astonished at the sight, as well he might be. The desert was as empty as ever, and there was no sign of anything in the rocky hills to the south that might have excited their alarms.

"Thet's jes' it," said Pete. "What is the matter with 'em? They ain't actin' up thet er way fer nuthin', you kin bet."

"Something must have scared them," said Jack. "Maybe it was those rocks you were throwing down."

"No, it warn't that, son. Ole One Spot he looked up here a minute ago, and giv' his eye a knowin' wink, as much as ter say: 'Go ahead; I know you won't hurt us.' No, siree; it's suthin' they've smelled out, er seen, that's given 'em the scare of their young lives."

"Maybe it was something on the other side of the mesa. Let's go and look," cried Jack.

Followed by the others, he ran across the flat summit, but an earnest inspection of the surroundings on that side failed to reveal any explanation for the animals' sudden terror. For all the strange objects that lay about them, they might have been in the middle of a desolate ocean.

"No wonder they call this the Haunted Mesa," snorted Pete. "I tell you, perfusser, ther sooner you git them thar measurements a-measured, and we're hiking out of this neck of the woods, the better I'll be pleased. 'Tain't natural, all these queer goings on."

"Maybe a coyote or something scared them," suggested Ralph.

"And them used ter seeing 'em every day," scoffed Pete. "Guess again, son. It takes something with hoofs, horns and red fire about it to scare a burro, and you kin bet your Sunday sombrero on that."

"Well, I propose that we adjourn the meeting till after dinner," laughed Jack; "all in favor, will signify by saying 'aye.'"

The chorus that answered him left no doubt of "the sense of the meeting," and a rapid descent of the mysterious mesa was begun. A good meal was not long in being prepared, thanks to

Coyote Pete's skill as a camp cook. Seated over their dinner, the main topic of conversation was naturally the unaccountable occurrence of the morning. But although a score of explanations were advanced, nobody could hit on one that seemed to fit the case.

"This water is singularly pure and sparkling,"' said the professor finally, by way of changing the subject, and holding up his full tin cup.

"Yep; I remember hearing old cowmen say that there's no water in New Mexico any better than this from the Haunted Mesa," said Pete, stretching himself out, and lighting his inevitable after-meal-time pipe. "Though that ain't sayin' a heap," he admitted.

"Wonder how those old what-you-may-call-ums ever managed to dig such a well?" questioned Ralph.

"Comes to my mind now," said Pete, "that it ain't exactly a well. An old Injun that used ter hang around with the Flying Z outfit tole us oncet that thar was a subterranean river flowed under here, and that once upon a time afore all the country dried up, considerable more water came to the surface here than there does now."

"A subterranean river?" asked the professor, at once interested.

"Yes, sir," rejoined Pete, "and not the only one in the West, either. There's one in Californy that flows underground fer purty near fifty miles, as I've heard tell."

"This is most remarkable," said the professor. "I, too, have heard of subterranean rivers in this part of the world, but I have never had the opportunity to explore one. Did this Indian you speak of ever tell you where this river emerges?"

"He said it come out some place across the frontier in Chihuahua; I don't jest rightly recollect where," said Pete carelessly, as if the subject did not interest him much, as indeed it did not.

"I don't see what use a subterranean river is to anybody, anyhow," he went on. "If it was on top, now, it might be some use."

"But this is most interesting," protested the professor, while the boys lay about with their chins propped in their hands in intent attitudes. "Then, too, if this river exists, perhaps it is even navigable."

"Why, professor!" exclaimed Jack. "Is it not possible that it was to this river that those drawings of boats that interested and puzzled you so much had reference?"

"Quite possible, my boy," agreed the man of science.

"I wish we could find some way of getting down into it," said Ralph wistfully, poking at the ground, as if he thought he might force an entrance that way.

"Thar you go," laughed Pete. "Giv' you boys a cayuse, an' you'll ride him to death. I jes' mentioned that a lying, whisky-drinking old Injun had sprung a pipe-dream about a lost river, and thar you go navagatin' it in a Coney Island steamboat."

The boys could not help bursting into a laugh at the cow-puncher's whimsical way of talking. The professor joined in, too, for none realized better than he did that for a moment he, too, had been quite carried away by the idea.

"I expect that it is as you say, Pete," he agreed. "These Indians are most unreliable people. If anybody was to believe all the weird legends an Indian tells him, he would spend the best part of his life on wild-goose chases. Why, the Indians of the Mojave desert in California can even tell a circumstantial story about a buried city of Mojave. According to their contention, a great flood, occurring long ago, wiped it out and buried it in the sands of the desert."

"Has any one ever tried to find it?" asked Jack.

"Many expeditions have been fitted out for the purpose, my boy," was the rejoinder, "but so far no trace has ever been found of it, and it is, no doubt, like the lost river of which Pete was telling us, a mere myth."

"I didn't say it was a miff," protested Pete. "I jes' said I didn't believe it."

The remainder of that afternoon was spent in making more measurements and sketches of the interesting mesa, and the boys, on their own account, conducted a search for a possible entrance to the lost river. But, as may be supposed, they found none.

"I guess as romance-seekers we are not a success," said Jack, as at sun-down they prepared to quit. "Just think, what a proud bunch we'd have been if we could say we - The Border Boys - discovered the lost river of the mesa dwellers."

"We might be a sorry bunch, too," amended the practical Walt. "I tell you, Jack, I don't want anything to do with lost rivers, especially when they are underground."

"Walt, the spirit of adventure is lacking in you," laughed Jack. "You'd never make a Don Quixote -"

"A donkey who?" asked Walt innocently.

"Oh, you're the limit," chuckled Ralph, going off into a roar of laughter at the ranch boy's expense.

That evening the animals' pasture was changed to the opposite side of the mesa, where they could find fresh grass. The camp, however, was left as it was. After supper watches were assigned, as usual, the latter part of the night guardianship falling to

Coyote Pete and Jack once more. When, soon after midnight, Walt and Ralph Stetson aroused them, there was nothing much to report except that One Spot had engaged in a spirited kicking match with his brethren. Outside of that, all had been, to quote Walt:

"Quiet along the Mesomac."

"We'll patrol round the whole mesa," said Coyote Pete, as he and Jack shouldered their rifles, "meeting by the stock on the other side."

After a few words more, the two sentries strode off into the darkness in different directions, meeting, as arranged, by the stock. Neither had anything to report, and in this way they kept up the night watch for an hour or more. They had met for the sixth time by the tents containing their sleeping comrades, when from the opposite side of the mesa came a shrill neigh of terror, followed by sounds of wild galloping and snorting.

"Something's up!" shouted Pete, as, with his rifle in readiness and followed closely by Jack, he tore around the mesa to ascertain the cause of the trouble.

As the two sentries emerged into view of the spot in which the stock had been tethered, they came upon a spectacle which, for a moment, caused them to recoil as abruptly as if a deep canyon had suddenly opened up before them.

CHAPTER VII

WHAT CAME ACROSS THE DESERT

That which brought the two - the plainsman and the lad - to such an amazed halt was nothing more nor less than the sight of the huge forms which had appeared to Jack in the sand-storm and which had given them such an alarm the night before, and which doubtless, as they now viewed it in a flash of intuition, had almost stampeded the stock while their owners were exploring the top of the mesa. But Coyote Pete was not the man to remain long rooted in astonishment.

With one quick jerk, he raised his rifle, and a vivid spatter of fire followed. As the report died out, one of the great forms sank to the ground with a scream that sounded almost human. The others glided off in the same direction as they had the night before, and vanished in the same mysterious way, before the thunderstruck Jack could get a shot at them.

"They're real, at any rate," exclaimed Coyote Pete, showing in his tone of relief, that until the great shadowy mass had sunk before his bullet, he had had some doubts of that fact.

"W-w-w-w-what is it?" came a frightened voice at their elbows, and, looking around, they saw the professor, in pajamas striped like a barber's pole, gazing apprehensively about him. Close behind him came Ralph Stetson and Walt, their weapons clasped determinedly, and evidently ready to face whatever emergency the sudden shot had betokened.

"Yes, what is it - Indians or bears?" demanded Ralph, entirely forgetful of the fact that bears are not wont, as a rule, to roam the barren desert.

"Dunno, but we'll see in a minute," said the cow-puncher, in answer to the excited questions. Followed by the rest, he made his way forward to where the great bulk that he had shot lay still and motionless on the ground. Even Jack owned to a slight feeling of apprehension as they neared the great form, - harmless as, whatever it might be, it had now become.

As for the stock, they were still plunging wildly about and snorting in a terrified fashion, and, had it not been for their stout raw-hide tethers, they would undoubtedly have stampeded.

Drawing a match, Pete held it high as he neared the stricken bulk outstretched before them. The next minute he gave an astonished cry:

"A camel!"

"A *what*!" gasped the entire group in unison.

"Jes' what I said, a backterian camel," reiterated Pete, striking another match.

They could all see then that he spoke the truth, astounding as it seemed. The creature that lay still before them, a bullet through its brain, was a veritable, undoubted specimen of the Bactrian species.

"But - but - great heavens!" cried Jack, hardly able to believe his eyes, "how, - what -"

"What on earth is a camel doing out here on the New Mexican desert?" the professor finished for him.

"Going eight days without a drink," suggested Ralph in an

undertone; but none of the party was in a mood for humor just then.

It was Pete who solved the mystery.

"I've got it," he exclaimed, "and I'm a plum-busted idjut not to have thought uv it afore; I've hearn about 'em often enough. This here backterian camel must be one of that bunch of Circus Jesse's."

"Circus Jesse! Who was he, or she?" asked Jack.

"Why, he was a feller what owned a big eastern circus, but owned a ranch out here as well. It struck him one time that if camels was good for transportation purposes over the Sahara desert they ought ter be just as good here. So, what does he do but start a camel express from Maguez ter Amadillo over the border, with some of the backterians frum his circus."

"And didn't it work?" asked Ralph.

"No. That is, it did fer a while, till ther novelty wore off, and then folks went back ter ther old reliable mule or burro. Circus Jesse, he got so blamed sore, that one fine day he turned the whole shootin' match of his backterians loose, and packin' his trunk, let the country, and resolved in futur' ter stick ter his circus."

"Was that long ago?" asked Jack. "I shouldn't have thought the creatures would have lived long without being recaptured."

"It's about five years since Jesse got out, I reckon," rejoined Pete, "an' fer a while camel-hunting was a popular sport. By an' by, however, they got so wary no one could get near 'em, and, except fer a scare they'd throw inter a prospector now and ag'in, we never heard no more of 'em. I'd clean fergotten all about 'em, till I made this one inter cold backterian meat."

"I suppose they found food and water here and regarded the

Mesa as their own property," declared Jack.

"That's about it. This is a place that's seldom visited, and I guess they just figgered out that they'd found a happy home."

"But what became of the rest of them?" asked Ralph, who had been apprised by Jack of the strange vanishment of the dead creature's mates.

"Must uv gone down that draw I noticed frum ther top uv ther mesa to-day," explained Pete. "Yer see, frum here, it would look as if they vanished inter the solid earth when they entered it, bein' as how you can't see there's any kind of a gully there till you get up high."

The next morning this was found to be the true explanation. Tracks on the bottom of the gully showed plainly how the strange desert wanderers had effected their disappearance in such a startling manner. But it was some time before Pete could sit down to a meal without being reminded of his "fire-spouting spook," which had cast such alarm into the camp the first night. The boys spent a week more at the mesa, during which time Professor Wintergreen obtained voluminous notes on one of the most interesting specimens of its kind in the south-west.

The days passed tranquilly, and, with the exception of the duty of removing the carcass of the dead camel, nothing to interrupt the routine of survey work occurred. The mates of the dead beast had evidently decided not to revisit their pasture grounds, for they did not put in a reappearance.

"Well, boys," said the professor one morning when they were all gathered at the summit of the mesa, "I guess that to-morrow morning we can say good-by to the scene of our rather tame adventures. My work is complete."

"How about the subterranean river?" asked Ralph, but a howl of derision from the others silenced him.

"Subterranean fiddlestick," burst out Jack, but the professor silenced him.

"The existence of such a stream is not so improbable as you seem to think," he said, "and Master Ralph is to be commended for his enterprising desire to locate it, but I think that our investigations have shown that if such a river ever did exist and the mesa dwellers had access to it, that the entrance, wherever it might have been, has vanished long ages ago."

Pete had taken no part in this conversation, but had wandered about the top of the mesa rather aimlessly, from time to time looking sharply at the surroundings beneath him in the alert manner of one whose life has been passed in the open places.

Suddenly he gave a quick exclamation and pointed off into the north-west.

"Look! Look there!" he exclaimed, riveting his eyes on something his keen vision had sighted, but which remained as yet invisible to the boys.

"What's coming - another storm?" asked Ralph.

"I don't know what it is yet," rejoined the other in a strangely uneasy tone, "it looks like - like -"

"A pillar of dust," exclaimed Jack, who had by this time sighted it, too, and had come to the aid of the unimaginative plainsman.

"So it does," cried the others, who now, with the exception of the short-sighted professor, could also see the approaching dust-cloud.

"What can it be?" wondered Walt, peering eagerly in its direction.

"Somebody riding. Several of 'em, I should say, by the dust

they're raising," rejoined Pete bluntly.

The boys exchanged quick glances. Somebody riding across that arid waste? Their destination could only be the mesa, then, but who could it possibly be?

Had they been able to solve the riddle at that instant, they would have scattered pell-mell for their ponies, and made the best of their way from the Haunted Mesa, but, not being endowed with anything more than ordinary sensibilities, it was, of course, impossible for them to realize the deadly peril that was bearing down upon them in that dust-cloud.

"I can see things more clearly now," cried Jack, as for an instant a vagrant desert air blew aside the dust-cloud and revealed several riders, surrounding some cumbersome, moving object in their midst.

"There's a wagon!" he cried, "a big one, too, and surrounded by horsemen. What can it mean?"

"That we'd better be skedaddling as quick as possible," shot out Pete, brusquely.

The professor, who had wandered away from the group and was down inside the hollow altar, was hastily summoned and apprised of the strange approach of the mysterious cavalcade.

"Why, bless me, boys, what can it mean?" he cried, nimbly attempting a flying leap over the edge of the altar in his haste to ascertain for himself the nature of the approaching party.

Suddenly, however, as his feet touched the top, and he was scrambling over, he gave a sharp cry and fell back within the altar with a gasp of pain.

"Are you hurt?" asked Jack, running to the side of the ancient place of sacrifice.

The professor lay prostrate within. His face was white and set and beads of sweat stood out on his forehead.

"My - my ankle," he groaned. "I broke it some time ago, and in hurrying to clamber over the top of the altar I fear I have snapped it again. Oh!"

He gave a heartrending groan of pain. The boys stood stricken with consternation. It was going to be a long and difficult task to get the professor out of his present predicament, and there seemed need for haste.

"Here, put this under your head," said Jack, stripping off his jacket hastily, and throwing it within, "I'll tell Coyote Pete about your accident, and we can get remedies from the packs."

But when Jack turned, only Ralph and Walt stood beside him. The sturdy cow-puncher had vanished.

"He's gone to get the glasses," explained Walt.

Presently Coyote Pete, very much out of breath from his dash down the path and up again, stood beside them. He had the glasses in his hand, and lost no time in applying them to his eyes. He had not had them there two minutes when he gave a quick exclamation and turned hastily to the boys.

"Lie down; lie down, every one of you," he ordered sharply.

They lost no time in obeying, as they knew that the old plainsman must have an excellent reason for such a command. The next instant Pete himself followed their example. Crouching low, he once more peered through the glasses above the edge of the cup-like depression.

"Who are they?" asked Jack in a low voice, wriggling his way to Pete's side.

"I'm not sure yet, but they are all armed. I caught the flash of sunlight on their rifles. If they are Mexican insurrectos, we are in a bad fix."

"Mexicans! What would they be doing this side of the border?"

"That remains to be seen. But I don't like the looks of it."

"Suppose they are Mexicans, Pete, would they do us any harm?"

"That depends a whole lot on whether they are on lawful business or not."

"You mean -"

"That I don't like the looks of it. If there's an insurrection in Mexico, those fellows are after no good on this side of the border. They may be some band of cut-throats, who are taking advantage of the disturbances to raise Cain."

"Good gracious," exclaimed Jack, "and the professor's just injured himself so that we can't move him for some time anyhow."

Coyote Pete turned sharply on the boy.

"What's he done?"

"Broken his ankle, or, at any rate, seriously sprained it."

Pete's rejoinder to this was a long whistle of dismay. He said nothing, however, but once more applied the glasses to his eyes. Jack saw him gnaw his moustache, as he gazed out over the desert. The dust-cloud was quite close now - not more than a mile away. The boys, with their naked eyes, could easily catch the moving glint of metal.

"Well, Pete, what do you think?" inquired Jack eagerly, as the cowpuncher at length set down the glasses.

"That we're in Dutch," was the expressive rejoinder.

CHAPTER VIII

THE DARK FACE OF DANGER

"Are we in actual danger?"

It was Ralph who put the question. The Eastern lad looked rather white under his tan. Walt, however, seemed as imperturbable as ever, and gazed out at the approaching horsemen with no more sign of emotion than a tightening of the lips.

Coyote Pete's reply was a curious one. He handed the boy the glasses, and said curtly:

"Take a squint fer yourself."

Ralph gazed long and earnestly. Pete talked the while in low undertone.

"Do you recognize him - that fellow on the big black horse? I'd know that horse ten miles away, even if I didn't know the man. He's -"

"Black Ramon de Barros!" burst from the Eastern lad's astounded lips, while the others gave a sharp gasp of surprise.

"That's the rooster. Here, Jack; take a look."

The boy, as you may suppose, lost no time in applying the glasses to his own eyes. Viewed through the magnifying medium, a startling moving-picture swung into focus.

Surrounding a big, covered wagon, of the prairie-schooner type, were from ten to a dozen wild-looking Mexicans, their straggling elf-locks crowned by high-peaked sombreros, and their serapes streaming out wildly about them, whipped into loose folds by the pace at which they rode. As Coyote Pete had said, there was little difficulty for any one who had seen him once, in recognizing Black Ramon de Barros. His magnificent black horse - the same on which he had escaped from the old mission - made him a marked man among a thousand. The wagon was drawn by six mules, and driven by a short, stocky, little Mexican. The horsemen seemed to act as escort for it. Evidently they had no fear of being observed by hostile eyes, for, as they advanced, they waved their rifles about their heads and yelled exultingly.

Fortunately for the party on the summit of the mesa, their stock was tethered on the opposite side of the formation to that on which the cavalcade was approaching. Thus, Black Ramon and his men could not see that the mesa was occupied. Jack caught himself wondering, though, how long it would be before, and what would happen when, they did.

"Have you got any plan in your head?" he asked, turning to Pete, as he laid the glasses down. But for once, to his dismay, the old plainsman seemed fairly stumped. The danger had come upon them so suddenly, so utterly unexpectedly, that it had caught them absolutely unprepared. They had not even a rifle with them on the mesa summit, and it was now too late to risk exposing themselves by descending for weapons. There was nothing to do, it seemed, but powerlessly to await what destiny would bring forth.

"You boys get back to the altar. You can act as company fer the profusser, and it will be a snug hiding-place in case of trouble," whispered Pete. "I wish to goodness we'd brought the stock up inside the mesa, and then those fellows might never have discovered we were here. I don't see how they can help it, as things are, though."

"They'll be bound to see our footmarks in the assembly hall," said Jack.

"Not bound to, lad," rejoined Pete. "You see, they may be only going to make this a watering-place fer their stock, and then press right on."

"Press right on across that rocky range yonder?"

"Hum," resumed Pete, "that's so. They couldn't very well get that wagin across that, could they?"

"Whatever do you suppose they've got a wagon for, at all?" asked Jack.

"I've got my own ideas, lad, and I'll find out afore long if I'm right. Now, you and the other boys get back in that altar. If it gets too hot here, I'll jump in and join you. If the worst comes to the worst, we ought to be able to lay hid in there fer a while."

"In the meantime what are you going to do?"

"Keep my eyes and ears open. There's something mighty strange about this whole thing."

The boys knew that obedience to Pete's commands was about the best thing they could do at the moment, so they hastened to conceal themselves within the altar, which afforded a comfortable hiding-place, even if it was a trifle hot. The poor professor was in great pain from his ankle, but Jack, after as able an examination as he could give the injured member, was unable to find that it was anything more than a severe sprain.

It did not take the professor long to become acquainted with what had happened within the last fifteen minutes, and, in his anxiety over the outcome of their situation, his pain was almost forgotten.

"If we only had the rifles," he breathed in such a savage voice that had the circumstances been different the boys could have smiled at the odd contrast between his mild, spectacled countenance and his bloodthirsty words.

It seemed hours, although in reality not more than half an hour elapsed, before Coyote Pete returned. His reappearance was not an orderly one. Instead, he landed in the interior of the altar in one bound. His face was streaming with sweat, and he looked anxious and worried.

"What news?" asked Jack.

"The worst," was the rejoinder.

"Have they found our camp?"

"Not yet, but that's only a question of a few minutes now. At present they are unhitching and cooking a meal. Luckily the shade at this time of day lies to the north-west of the mesa, so that they may not explore the other side for some time."

"Let us hope not. But what have you found out about them? What are they doing here?"

"Just what I suspicioned. They are a part of a gang of gun-runners."

"Gun-runners?"

"Yes. From listening to their conversation, I have found out that this insurrection's a heap worse than we ever supposed. Half of Chihuahua is up in arms ag'in the government, and they are plotting to blow up railroad bridges, cut wires, and paralyze the country generally. Then they are goin' ter raid all the American mines and get the gold."

"Why, dad's mine's in Chihuahua, close to the border," gasped Jack.

"I know it. I heard that greaser ragamuffin, Black Ramon, mention his name. Your dad's the first one they're goin' after -"

"The scoundrels."

"They owe him a grudge, you know, and now's their chance to get even."

"Do they know that dad is in Mexico now?"

"I didn't hear that. All I found out was what I told you, and that, as I said, they are running guns across the border. That wagon's loaded up with machine-guns in heavy cases. They are labeled as agricultural machinery, and were taken off the train by white accomplices seventy miles or more from here. They chose this part of the border, I guess, as even Uncle Sam would never suspect any one of trying ter get guns over them hills yonder."

"Well, they can't take a wagon over those rocky, desolate places. How are they going to get them across, do you suppose?" asked the professor, his pain almost forgotten in the tense interest of the moment.

"That's just the funny part uv it," said Pete; "they never mentioned the mountains. You don't suppose there's any other way they could get 'em over the border, do you?"

"Maybe they have an airship," suggested Walt Phelps.

"Maybe," said Pete quite gravely, "I wouldn't put nothin' past a greaser."

"Hush!" exclaimed Ralph suddenly, "somebody's coming."

With beating hearts they sank into absolute silence. The three

Fremont B. Deering

boys crouched at one end of the hollow altar, the professor and Coyote Pete bundled together into as small a space as possible at the other.

Voices, conversing in Spanish, could now be heard, and, from the inflection, the boys judged that whoever was talking was very much astonished over something.

"I recognize that voice," said Jack suddenly, in a low whisper, "it's Ramon de Barros."

The other two boys nodded. Ralph Stetson's heart beat so hard and fast that it fairly shook his frame. Truly the predicament of the party was a terrible one. Discovery by as wolf-hearted a band of ruffians - if they were all like their leader - as ever infested the border, was inevitable within the next few minutes. Taking into consideration their connection with Black Ramon in the past, it was unlikely in the extreme that any mercy would be shown them. Never had any of them looked so closely into the dark face of danger.

Suddenly the listeners, crouching in their hiding-place, heard a shout of astonishment from the Mexicans.

"They've seen our camp over the edge of the mesa!" exclaimed Pete in a low, tense voice; "in another minute they'll start looking for us."

As he spoke, the voice which Jack had recognized as Black Ramon's, uttered a crisp, curt command of some sort. The lads could hear footsteps hurrying hither and thither. Without doubt, the order that meant their probable doom had just been given.

"I can't stand this a minute longer," cried Ralph suddenly. The boy's eyes were blazing wildly. Clenching his fist, he sprang to his feet.

"Come back here, you blockhead," snapped Jack, tugging his

friend down. Ralph came backward sprawling, and landed in a heap in Jack's lap, knocking Walt Phelps with him. Together the three boys were tangled in a struggling heap.

"Get up," whispered Jack. "They'll hear us. You -"

He stopped short. All at once an astonishing - an incredible thing - had happened. The floor beneath them, - the solid floor, as it had seemed, - began to tremble.

Before any of the amazed lads could utter a word, the foundation upon which they rested tipped, and, with a loud, ringing cry of terror from Ralph, they were plunged out of the sunlight into blackness as impenetrable as the pocket of Erebus.

CHAPTER IX

IN THE MESA DWELLERS' BURIAL GROUND

Down, down, they plunged, bumping and scraping painfully in the darkness. Terror had deprived them of speech or the power of uttering a sound, or they would have shouted. As it was, however, when they finally landed in a heap on some hard surface at the foot of the steep declivity down which they had fallen, it was some seconds before any of them breathed a word. Then it was Jack who spoke.

"Fellows!"

"Yes, Jack." The rejoinder came out of the darkness in Walt Phelps' voice.

"Ralph, are you there?"

"No; I'm dead. That is, I feel as if every bone in my body had been broken. What in the name of Old Nick has happened?"

"Thank goodness there are no bones broken," breathed Jack thankfully, as Ralph spoke, "as to what happened, you can take your own guess on it. My idea is that there was some sort of hinged trap-door at the bottom of that altar, and that when our combined weight came upon it at the time I pulled Ralph down, the blamed old thing tipped and dumped us down in here."

"That's my idea, too," chimed in Walt. "Can't account for it in any other way. But what is 'here'? Where are we?"

"You can answer that as well as I can," was the rejoinder. "Anybody got a match? Oh, here; all right, I've got some, plenty in fact - a whole pocketful."

Jack struck a lucifer, and as its yellow glare lit up their surroundings, they could not repress a cry of astonishment. They had landed at the foot of a steep flight of stairs, at the summit of which they correctly surmised was the trap-door through which they had been so startlingly dumped.

"Good gracious, did we fall down all those?" murmured Ralph, rubbing his elbow painfully.

"Guess so. I know I feel as if I'd been monkeying with a buzz-saw," same [Transcriber's note: came?] from Walt Phelps.

"Well, fellows," said Jack, as the light died out, "the question now before us is, what are we going to do?"

"Try to get out again," said the practical Walt Phelps.

"All right, Walt. Then we'd better remount those steps - slower than we came down them - and try to reopen that trap-door. We can't leave Pete and the injured professor like this."

The boys clambered up the steps without difficulty. They were deep and shallow, and were cut out of the living rock. At the head of the stairs, however, a disappointment awaited them. Try as they would, they could not discover any means of reopening the stone trap-door in the floor of the hollow altar. Apparently, after dumping them through, it had closed as hermetically as before.

The flickering light of the matches from Jack's store illuminated looks of despair on their faces as they realized that they were trapped.

"Try pounding on it and shouting," suggested Ralph.

Although Jack deemed it of little use, he and Walt followed this suggestion, and together the three boys beat and hammered on the massive stone above them till their hands were raw. There was no response, however. Apparently the stone was too thick for a sound to penetrate to the outer air. Terror, that was almost panic, seized Walt and Ralph, as they realized that they were prisoners in this hermetically sealed dungeon. Worse than prisoners, in fact. Prisoners had food and at least hope. They, unless they could find a way out, were buried alive. Even Jack's stout heart experienced a deadly feeling of depression, as he realized this. He concealed his despair from his companions, however, and, with all the cheerfulness he could muster, addressed them in the darkness. Matches had now grown too precious to squander.

"Well, fellows, we've got to find another way out."

"Oh, it's no good," moaned Ralph despairingly, "we're doomed to die here. We might as well sit down and wait for death to come."

"Say," cut in Jack briskly, "if it was light enough to see, I'd give you a good licking. Doomed to die, indeed! Not much. It's a cinch, isn't it, that if there is an entrance to this place there must be an outlet, too? Very well, then," he hurried on, without waiting for an answer, "let's find that outlet."

The logic of this speech might be questioned, but of its good sense, under the circumstances, there was no doubt.

"You're right, Jack," said Ralph. "I'm ashamed of myself for doing the baby act. Come on, let's set out at once."

"That's the talk," said Walt heartily; "if there's a way out, we'll find it."

"And if not?" asked Ralph, his spirits flagging again.

"We'll discuss that later," declared Jack briskly.

Returning again to the landing - if such it might be called - upon which they had terminated their abrupt descent into the interior of the mesa, some more of the precious matches were lit. As the last flickered out, the boys fancied that some feet from them they could see a black mouth, like the entrance of a tunnel, or rather a continuation of the one into which they had been thrown.

"Come on, boys," exclaimed Jack. "It's the only thing to do. We can't turn back, and, as Pete says, 'there ain't nothing to do but go ahead.'"

Not without some misgivings did the three lads plunge forward in the darkness, feeling their way with outstretched hands as they entered the tunnel. A close, musty smell, as of things long mildewed and moulded, filled the air, and an oppressive silence lay on everything. Unconsciously, since entering this place, their conversation had been all in whispers.

The tunnel they were now traversing was bored on a pretty steep down grade. So steep, in fact, that Jack concluded, after about a quarter of an hour of slow and cautious traveling, that they must be below the level of the desert. For the last few minutes they had been conscious of a peculiar thing. This was that the silence of the tunnel had given place to a deep-throated roaring, not unlike the voice of a blast furnace. Where it came from, or what it was, they had no idea. It was a most peculiar sound, though, steady as a trade-wind, and seeming to fill the whole place with its deep vibrations.

"What can it be?" gasped Walt, as they paused by common consent to listen.

"Maybe the wind roaring by the entrance to this place," suggested Jack hopefully.

This thought gave them new courage, and, on Ralph's

suggestion, Jack struck another match from his store. As it flared up, they all three recoiled with expressions of dismay.

At their very feet - so close that the tips of their boots almost projected over it - was a deep chasm. The black profundity of it loomed in front of them gapingly. A few paces more, and they would have been precipitated into the abyss. Jack, suppressing a shudder, leaned forward and held the match as far over the edge as he dared. As the depths of the great crevasse were illuminated by a feeble flame, he shrank back with a sharp intake of his breath.

The place was a charnel house!

No mystery now as to what had become of the human remains of the grisly sacrifices of the ancient mesa dwellers. There, piled in that dark chasm beneath them, were great piles of decaying bones and gleaming skulls. Hundreds of them extended toward the surface in a ghastly pyramid. No wonder the underground place into which they had penetrated smelled musty and unpleasant.

"It is the mesa dwellers' burial ground!" exclaimed Ralph in a quavering voice, as, clinging to Jack's arm, he bent forward.

"Yes," rejoined Walt with a shudder, "and but for Providence, we should have plunged downward into it ourselves."

"Ugh!" exclaimed Jack, in a voice filled with repulsion. "Don't let's think of it. See, the path takes a turn here. Come on, let's go ahead, but follow me closely and keep in to the wall."

"Not likely to take any chances of missing the road, after seeing that," spoke up Walt, as once more the three youths, who had been so strangely plunged into this predicament, began to tread the subterranean regions once more.

As you may imagine, they went with due caution. But no more dangers menaced them, and as they progressed the path began to widen. All the time, however, the strange roaring sound had been growing louder, until now it had attained almost deafening proportions. Still they had come upon no explanation of what it could be. Jack had privately co ncludedit to be the sound of the wind, forcing its way into some crevice. This theory seemed to be the more tenable as the last match which he had struck had only been kept alight with difficulty, so strong had been the draught that now puffed up toward them.

Far from alarming them, however, this gave them renewed hope. It meant that, in all probability, they were nearing an outlet of the strange underground place. Had it not been for the predicament in which they had left the professor and Coyote Pete, the three lads would have felt a real interest in exploring the cavern, now that they had grown accustomed to their surroundings. So far as they had been able to make out, the tunnel they had been treading was partially the work of human hands and partially the work of Nature. The great rift in which lay the accumulation of human remains was evidently the result of some volcanic upheaval. The path, however, was so graded and formed that there seemed no reason to doubt that it had, at one time, been made by the ancient mesa dwellers.

"Seems to me we ought to find out what that roaring sound means before we go any farther," suggested Ralph suddenly.

"That's a fine Irish bull," laughed Jack. "How are we going to find what it is unless we do go farther?"

"That's so," agreed Ralph, somewhat abashed. "Come on, then."

A few paces more brought them to an abrupt turn in the path, as they could feel by their constant touching of the inner wall.

"Better strike another match," said Walt.

"Yes; here goes," agreed Jack. Both boys shouted, to make themselves heard above the now thunderous roaring of the strange noise.

A shout of surprise that rose even above the mysterious roaring, followed the striking of the match. Beyond the turn the path took a steep drop downward, and beyond that - the boys could hardly believe their eyes as they gazed - was the glint of rushing water.

"The subterranean river!" was the amazed cry that broke from the lips of all three.

CHAPTER X

A NEW MEXICAN STYX

"The subterranean river!"

The words echoed back weirdly from the vault-like chamber into which they had now penetrated, and at the bottom of which the stream, upon which the light of the match had glistened, flowed rapidly. Within this spacious place the noise was not nearly so loud as it had been when confined in the narrow tunnel, which, in fact, acted muc h as aspeaking-tube would have done.

"It can't be!" gasped Ralph, unwilling to believe his own eyes.

"But it is," cried Jack, as, all thoughts of their predicament forgotten in this strange discovery, they made lavish use of their matches on gaining the edge of the stream. The river was about twenty feet in width, and they speedily saw that the roaring sound they had heard during their progress through the tunnel was produced by a waterfall some distance above, over which the river plunged into a sort of basin at their feet.

But this was not the most astonishing thing they found in that first brief but comprehensive inspection. Affixed to the rocky wall at one side of the chamber was a large, bronze lamp. An eager overhauling of the utensil showed it to be filled with oil, and apparently it was not so very long since it had been lighted.

Fremont B. Deering

Hastily applying a match, Jack soon had the rocky chamber lighted, and they could now survey the place into which they had blundered, at their ease. In size it was about the same dimensions as the Council Hall of the mesa, which lay, they knew not how many feet, above them. The river roared down along one side of it, forming a deep, turbid pool just beneath the waterfall, by which it entered the place.

To their astonishment, the boys now spied in one corner of the chamber several empty boxes piled up. Remains of excelsior and sacking were within them, and they bore the stencilled marks, "Agricultural Machinery, With Care."

Instantly what Pete had related to him concerning the conversation of the men accompanying Black Ramon flashed into Jack's mind. Could it be possible that they had stumbled upon the place utilized by the gun-runners to convey their ammunition across the border? At this instant, there came a shout from Ralph, who had been peering about the place.

"A boat!"

"A what?" The incredulous cry burst from both Jack and Walt.

"It is a kind of a boat, anyhow. Come here, and look for yourselves."

Ralph was bending over the rocky marge of the subterranean river at a part of the chamber farthest removed from the waterfall. The water here flowed comparatively slowly, most of its force having been expended in the pool beneath the fall. Sure enough, Ralph had been right. Moored to the bank by two stout ropes attached to iron bars driven into the rock, was a boat - if such a name can be given to the flat-bottomed, floating appliance, upon which the thunderstruck boys gazed.

The boat, or rather float, was about twenty feet in length and some five feet in beam. It was not unlike, in fact, one of those shallow craft used by duck hunters, only it was square at each end. Evidently it would hold a considerable quantity of freight. More excelsior and burlap litter in the bottom of it showed that whatever had been the contents of the boxes, it had apparently been used to transport them.

"Boys, we've tumbled over the discovery of the age!" exclaimed Jack, in what was for him, a strangely excited voice.

The others were not less moved. Their eyes were round and their jaws dropped in incredulous wonderment, as they gazed before them.

"Will somebody please pinch me?"

It was Ralph who spoke, turning a countenance solemn and startled upon
his comrades.

"No need to do that, Ralph. You're wide-awake; make no mistake about that."

"But - but I don't understand," began Walt in a puzzled tone. "What is this place, what -"

"What is it?" echoed Jack. "It's the gun-runners' underground railroad. Can't you see it? This river, so the old Indian legend says, emerges across the border. In some way these Mexicans heard of it, and learned the secret of the hollow altar. No wonder the government has not been able to find out how the rebels got their arms across the border."

"Well, what are we going to do, now we've found it?"

Walt, the practical, propounded the query, as they stood there, half-stunned by the rapidity with which unheard-of events had happened within the last half-hour.

"Why, I - upon my word, I don't know," laughed Jack, brought up with a round turn by the hard-headed Walt.

"I do," rejoined Walt.

"What then?"

"Escape to the open air."

"You mean it?" Somehow, in his excitement, Jack had not gone as far as this daring suggestion. And yet it was, after all, the only thing to do. But suddenly another thought occurred to the boy.

"The professor and Coyote Pete, how can we leave them?"

"Well, we can't do them any good by remaining buried here, that's certain," replied Walt, in his sensible way.

Jack and Ralph nodded agreement.

"On the other hand, if this river really leads out into Mexico, we can take the subway to freedom and then, when we emerge, find out the best thing to do. Maybe we can fall in with some government troops or authorities of some kind."

"But suppose the insurrectos are in power wherever this river comes out?"

The question came from Ralph.

"We'll have to take chances on that, I suppose."

"Hark!" came suddenly from Jack.

Far back somewhere in the tunnels they had threaded they could hear loud shouts and cries. The sound of the pursuit boomed out even above the noise of the waterfall.

"They're after us!" exclaimed Jack.

"Shall we take the boat?" Walt's usually calm voice shook a

little as he asked the question.

"It's our only chance. Come on, in with you, Ralph."

Ralph hesitated no longer, but jumped into the little contrivance. A sort of oar lay in the bottom. He thrust it over the side.

"The water's only about three feet deep," he announced.

"So much the less chance of our being drowned," rejoined Jack.

The lad had his knife out - a heavy-bladed hunting weapon. As soon as all was ready he would cut the ropes and set the boat free on the turbulent current.

"All right!" cried Walt, as he clambered in and took his place by Ralph.

Jack gave a hasty look around, and the next instant made a flying leap into the little craft. So fast had Black Ramon and his followers taken up the trail after they had discovered that the boys had found the secret of the hollow altar, that they were already entering the chamber.

Ramon was in the lead. The glare of the lamp fell full on his parchment-like features, as with a roar of recognition, he sighted the boys.

Ping!

Something whizzed past Jack's ear, and, chipping the rock above, showered the occupants of the boat with fragments. The sharp report of the Mexican's revolver filled the place. With a quick movement, Jack slashed the rope nearest him. If he had not been in such a hurry, he would have seen that the other should have been severed first. As it was, he had cut the one that held the boat's bow to the stream. Instantly the flat-bottomed craft swung dizzily around, and still held by her stern mooring, dashed against the bank.

For a minute the boys feared she was stove in, but there was no time to waste on an examination.

Slash!

One stroke of the knife severed the remaining rope, already drawn as taut as a piano wire. But, as Jack's knife fell, the place became filled with shouts and confusion.

Ramon had been a little in advance of his men, and now they were all in the place. A second's glance showed them what had happened. Not only were the boys about to escape, but if they did not stop them the secret of their underground route across the border would be discovered, and its usefulness at an end.

No wonder they strained every nerve to reach the boys. Ramon himself had bounded to the side of the subterranean river as the boat swung round. As her gunwale had struck the bank, he had leaped aboard. But before he could use his revolver, Walt's powerful arm knocked the weapon out of his hand, and it fell on the bottom of the boat. With a snarl of rage, Ramon flashed round on the boy. But whatever the Mexican might have been able to do with knife or pistol, he was no match for the muscles of the American lad.

Walt fairly picked the lithe form of the gun-runner from the floor of the boat as Jack's knife fell across the remaining rope. With a splash and a loud cry, Ramon pitched overside into the stream. As he fell, though, he managed to clutch the side of the craft and he hung on, desperately endeavoring to draw himself up into the boat.

His followers, seeing what had happened, rushed down on them. A tempest of bullets rattled about the boys' heads as they felt the rope part. It was no moment for sentimental hesitation. Walt raised his foot, and the next instant brought his heavy boot down with crushing force on Ramon's clinging fingers.

With a yelp of pain, the fellow let go and was rolled over and over in the river, while half a dozen of his men waded in to rescue him.

"Yip-ee-ee-ee! We're off!" yelled Jack, with a true cowboy yell. The lad was carried away by the excitement and thrill of the adventure.

With a lurch and a bump, the frail craft carrying our three young friends shot forward. The lamp-lit panorama as Ramon, dripping and cursing, was hauled out of the water by his band, flashed before their eyes for a brief moment. The next instant dense darkness fell about them.

At what seemed to be a mile-a-minute pace they were hurried forward into the unknown.

CHAPTER XI

THE CAMP OF THE GUN-RUNNER

Jounced against the rough, rock walls, bumped over shoal places, and at times whirled almost broadside on by the swift current, the queer, flat-bottomed boat containing our three young friends was hurried through the darkness. It was the maddest ride any of them had ever taken, and, as we know, they had been through some thrilling experiences since they had first stood on the railroad station platform at Maguez. Had they known it, they could have controlled the boat more or less with the rough oar - the one with which Ralph had sounded the depth of the river - but, of course, they were inexpert in the management of such a craft. They could do nothing but keep still and trust to luck to bring them safely out of their extraordinary predicament.

After some ten minutes of this, the current seemed to slacken a little and the walls narrowed. Jack stretched out a hand and, to his astonishment, his fingers were swept along a rope stretched down the side of the tunnel. This solved a problem he had been revolving in his mind - namely, how did the Mexicans get their boat back after it had delivered its cargo of arms? The explanation was now a simple one. Evidently they hauled it back by the use of this rope. "It must have been hard work, though," thought Jack.

Conversation was impossible in the confines of the tunnel which, in places, was a mere tube in the rocks; the roar of the water was almost deafening. It was so black, too, that they could not see one another's faces. Of real alarm Jack did not feel much, and for an excellent reason. It was apparent that the Mexicans had used this underground route across the border many times, and, if they could make the passage - terrifying as it seemed - in safety, there was every reason to suppose that the boys could make it with the same security.

What worried Jack most about their situation proceeded from a far different cause. There was little reason to doubt that at the other end of the tunnel, wherever that might be, Black Ramon or his superiors, arming the insurrectionists, had guards posted to receive the smuggled guns. If no opportunity of escaping from the boat presented itself before they were hastened out of the exit of the tunnel, their situation would be just as bad as ever. Ramon would, of course, lose no time in following them up, either by a spare boat, which he might have had concealed in the vaulted chamber, or else on his fast, coal-black horse which he might ride across the rocky range, far above the subterranean stream.

In the event of their falling once more into the hands of Ramon, Jack could not repress a shudder as he thought of what the probable fate would be. Ugly stories had from time to time floated across the border concerning the manner in which Ramon, in his cattle-rustling days, dealt with his prisoners, - stories of torture and suffering that made one shudder even to listen to. If the apparent leader of the insurrectionist gun-runners had cause for animosity against the boys before, it was surely redoubled now. Not only had they accidentally penetrated the secret of the Haunted Mesa, but they had toppled the former leader of the cattle-rustlers ignominiously into the water, an insult which Jack knew the man's nature too well to suppose he would easily either forgive or forget.

In such gloomy reflections was he occupied when a sudden shout from the others roused him from his reverie, and, looking up, he saw that the tunnel through which the river flowed was growing higher, broader, and lighter. The darkness had now been exchanged for a sort of semi-gloom, in which the almost black rock gleamed wetly where the hurrying current of the stream had washed its base.

"We're near the end!" shouted Walt to the others.

Jack nodded. Suddenly his eye fell on Ramon's revolver, which lay at the bottom of the boat as it had fallen when he toppled overboard. One cartridge had been discharged, leaving but four good shells in the chamber, but in an emergency those four, the lad knew, would be better than no weapons at all. He regarded this as distinctly a piece of good luck - this finding of the pistol. He examined it and found that it was a heavy weapon of forty-four caliber.

Hardly had he had time to observe all this before the boat, without the slightest warning, shot out into daylight, very much as a railroad train emerges from a tunnel. A swift glance at their surroundings showed Jack that they had floated into a sort of natural basin amid some wild, bare-looking hills. The banks of this basin were clothed with a sort of wild oat and interspersed with a small blue wild flower. Here and there were clumps of chapparal. But what pleased the lad most was the fact that, although not far from them a rude hut stood upon the bank, there was so far no sign of human occupancy of the place.

Seizing the steering oar, Jack ran the boat up alongside a spot where the bank shelved gently down to the water's edge, and ran her, nose up, on the sand.

"Hoo -" began Ralph jubilantly, his spirits carrying him away, but Jack's hand was over his mouth in a second.

"The less noise we make the better," he breathed, stepping out of the boat on tiptoe and signing to the others to do the same. With scarcely a sound, they landed and stood at length on the grassy carpet sloping down to the sandy beach.

So far not a sound had proceeded from the hut Jack turned to his companions with a cautious gesture.

"Wait here while I investigate," he whispered, "and be ready to jump back into the boat and shove off at a minute's notice."

They nodded and turned to obey, as Jack, as silently as he could, crept on toward the hut, his revolver clasped ready for use at the slightest alarm. The Border Boy did not mean to be caught napping. In this manner he reached the wall of the hut nearest to the river, in which there was a small, unglazed window. Cautiously raising himself on tiptoe, Jack peered within.

In a rough chair, by a table covered with the untidy remains of a meal, was seated an elderly Mexican, as shriveled and brown as a dried bean. The regularity with which he was "sawing wood" showed that he was as sound asleep as it is possible for a man to be. Still Jack knew that there are men who sleep with one eye open, so he did not relax an iota of his vigilance as he crept around the corner of the house. On the opposite side he found a doorway, and, noiselessly gliding in, he had the pistol to the Mexican's ear before whatever dreams the man might have been having were even disturbed.

"Caramba, sanctissima! Santa Maria!" yelled the man, springing to his feet as if propelled by springs. But the uncomfortable sensation of the little circle of steel pressed to the nape of his neck brought him back again into the chair in a second, trembling like a leaf, and gazing in terror at the determined young figure standing over him.

"Keep quiet and I'll not hurt you," said Jack, adding as an afterthought: "Do you speak English?"

"Me spiggoty 'Merican," sputtered the trembling old Mexican.

"All right, Jose, then listen: Are there any horses here?"

The old man's eyes held a gleam of intelligence.

"Cavallo, senor. One, two, t'ree horse over heel."

"Oh, over the hill, are they?" said Jack to himself, then aloud: "You come and show them to me."

"Mocho easy to find," protested the Mexican.

Jack smiled to himself. He had been right, then. The old man was trying to trick him. Assuming a sterner air, he thundered out,

"Tell me where these horses are or I'll kill you!"

The threat proved effectual, as Jack had hoped it would. Dropping all his attempts at subterfuge, the Mexican told the boy that the horses were in a gully not a hundred feet from the house. On the Mexican being escorted there, still with the pistol held close to his head, his words were found to be true.

Three horses, ready saddled and bridled, stood in the gulch, apparently reserved for the use of any one about the camp who should need them in a hurry.

This much ascertained, Jack marched the Mexican back to the hut, where, with a rope, he leisurely proceeded to bind him. Then, amid the fellow's tears and supplications - for he evidently thought he was about to be killed - the boy marched him to the river bank. Walt and Ralph were naturally bubbling over with questions, but they said nothing as Jack sternly ordered the aged Mexican to board the boat.

There were more prayers and tears, but finally the shriveled old chap got on board, and the boys shoved him off. The current rapidly bore him off down the stream and presently he vanished between the two points of land through which the river made its way out of the basin.

"Well, he's off for a good, long ride," said Jack, as with howls and yells from its passenger the boat vanished from view.

"Why didn't you just bind him and leave him in the hut?" asked Ralph.

"Because Ramon may be along at any moment, and the old fellow might give him some information concerning us we wouldn't like to have published," was the rejoinder. "In that boat he is in no danger and will simply take a long and pleasant ride, and won't be in a position to do us any mischief when he is finally rescued."

The boys were full of admiration for Jack's strategy, and openly expressed their congratulations on the skillful way he had carried things through, but the lad waved them aside impatiently. Rapidly he told them that their best course was to get on horseback as soon as possible, and head away from the valley.

Some five minutes later three youthful figures mounted on a trio of splendid specimens of horse flesh, loped easily up a trail leading from the natural basin in the hills. In Jack's pocket, too, reposed a certain paper found on the table in the hut and signed with Ramon de Barros' name. With a vague idea that it might prove useful to him, the boy had appropriated it, and shoved it hastily in his pocket.

The summit of the basin reached, the boys found themselves not far from a broad, white road. The compass, which Jack still had on his wrist, showed the direction to be about due east and west. Crossing a stretch of grass, which separated them from the thoroughfare, the three young horsemen were soon standing on the ribbonlike stretch of white which wound its way through a country pleasantly green and fresh-looking after their sojourn in the desert.

"Looks like the promised land," cried Walt.

"I'll bet we're the first bunch to find the promised land via the underground railway," laughed Ralph, as they gazed about them, undecided in which direction to proceed.

CHAPTER XII

MADERO'S FLYING COLUMN

As they stood there, still undecided as to which direction to take, Jack's keen eyes detected, above a clump of trees some distance down the road to the west, a cloud of yellow dust rising. Evidently somebody was coming their way. The question was, who was it?

It might be some one of whom they could inquire the direction to the Esmeralda mine - for Jack had determined to seek out his father, knowing the mine could not be very far distant. Again it might be a band of insurrectos, in which case they would have jumped out of the frying pan into the fire with a vengeance.

"Shall we ride forward?" asked Walt, as Jack's lips tightened in deep thought.

The other boy pushed back his sombrero. Jack Merrill was only a lad, after all, and he found himself suddenly called upon to answer a question which might have stumped a grown man. The question, however, was decided for him, and by a means so utterly unexpected that it came near jolting the Border Boys out of their composure; for Jack, as they had ridden up from the river, had admonished his companions to keep cool minds and wits and stiff upper lips whatever happened. They were going into a country in which, from what they had been able to gather, the insurrectos were numerically and strategically strong. Their only safety, the lad argued with a wisdom beyond his years, was in facing emergencies as they came, without betraying by outward signs whatever of inward perturbation they might feel.

"I think we had better ride eastward, till we come to some village or town," Jack was beginning, in response to Walt's question, when a voice from behind suddenly hailed them in unmistakably American accents.

"Ah, here you are, gentlemen. We've been expecting you."

The boys wheeled to find that a horseman stood beside them. He had ridden almost noiselessly over the soft grass, which accounted for their not having heard his approach. Jack took in the new arrival's figure in a quick, comprehensive glance.

The man who now faced them was a stalwart-looking chap of about thirty. His face was bronzed and his eyes keen. The face of one who has lived much out of doors. His manner seemed frank and open - even hearty - but any one skilled in reading faces would have noted in the rather receding chin and the eyes set close together that, in spite of his apparent heartiness, the newcomer was a man of limited reliability. The sort of chap, in short, who, while fearless up to a certain point and adventurous to a degree, would yet in an extremity look out for "Number One."

As for his dress, it was much the same as the boys'. Sombrero, leather chaps well worn, blue shirt, and red neck handkerchief. Jack's keen eyes noted, too, that the pommel of his saddle bore some recent bullet scars, and that in two bearskin holsters reposed the formidable-looking butts of two heavy-caliber revolvers. The war-like note was further enhanced by the fact that across his saddle horn the new arrival carried a Remington rifle.

The boys' position was now an extraordinary one. Advancing toward them down the road, was, what they could now perceive to be, a considerable body of horsemen. As if this were not enough to raise a question of whether it was better to fly or remain where they were, here was this total stranger, perhaps an American, too, hailing them as if he knew them, or, at least, had expected to meet them there. Jack's mind was made up in a flash, but, even in the brief instant he hesitated, the stranger's keen, close-set eyes narrowed suspiciously.

"I'm not mistaken, am I? You expected to meet me here?"

"Yes, yes, of course," responded Jack quickly, and in as easy a tone as he could command; "I hope we're not late?"

"No; there comes Madero's flying column now. You couldn't have kept the appointment better if you had arranged to meet us at some spot in New York."

"I'm glad we're on time," said Jack, not knowing exactly what else to say.

The lad was thunderstruck, as well he might be, by the turn events were taking. He wished fervently, however, that they knew whom they were expected to be and why their coming had been awaited with such eagerness.

"I say, you know," rattled on the other, who seemed to be a pleasant natured enough chap, "that trip of yours through that hole in the ground has mussed you up a bit."

"It certainly has," agreed Jack, more and more mystified; "it's a pretty rough voyage."

"That's what, and going through that blamed trap in the Mesa, like a comedian in an extravaganza, isn't the least unpleasant part of it. It was a pretty slick trick of Ramon's to find that out, although, I guess, some old Indian gave him the tip."

"It's a great scheme," put in Walt Phelps, finding his tongue at last.

"You chaps are a good deal younger than I expected to find you," rattled on the stranger, "but I suppose you've seen lots of service."

"Yes, lots of it," put in Ralph, throwing some fervor into his tone. He felt that they had indeed, in the last few hours, seen service enough for a lifetime. Jack inwardly rejoiced as the others found their tongues. He had dreaded that the suddenness of the emergency might have proved too much for them. Both lads were rising to it gallantly, however. Now, if only he could find out who on earth they were supposed to be, they might yet escape from the predicament into which they had fallen.

"Now let's introduce ourselves," went on their new acquaintance, evidently not the least bit suspicious now. "My name's Bob Harding. Which of you chaps is Con Divver?"

"Right here," said Jack, motioning to Walt.

"And Jim Hickey and Ted Rafter?"

"I'm Jim and here is Ted," responded Jack, his heart beating like a trip hammer. It was a daring game they were playing.

"That's good. Now we all know each other. I think that Americans enlisted in this sort of service should be on good terms, don't you?"

"I certainly do," rejoined Jack warmly.

"Fine! I'll bet we'll make good messmates. And now here comes Madero himself. If you fellows will come with me, I'll introduce you in form. Do you 'spiggoty'?"

"Do we what?" asked Jack wonderingly.

"Spiggoty. Talk this greaser lingo?"

"Not very well, I'm afraid. Does the general talk English?"

"Well. He's a good fellow, too. You'll find out."

Thus rattling on, Bob Harding escorted the lads toward the van of the advancing horsemen. There were about a hundred in the troop, which Harding had referred to as a "Flying Column," and, although the horsemen were all apparently well armed, their appearance was ragged and wild in the extreme. They had evidently seen some hard fighting. Here and there could be seen men with bandaged heads or limbs, while their high conical-crowned hats were in some cases drilled, like beehives, with bullet holes. In color, the insurrecto leader's followers ranged from a delicate cream to a dark, reddish-brown, almost the coppery hue of a red Indian. In all, they formed as ferocious and formidable-looking a troop of horsemen as the Border Boys had ever set eyes on.

Madero himself, a rather sad-faced man of past middle age, rode in advance, surrounded by several officers, the latter having red flannel chevrons attached to their buckskin coats by safety pins. The famous insurrecto leader raised his hat with Mexican courtesy as the newcomers approached. Bob Harding drew himself up in his saddle and gave a military salute which the general stiffly returned. The boys, taking their cue from their new acquaintance, followed his example.

"I am afraid that your first experience with the insurrectos was a rough one, senores," said the general, with one of his sad smiles, using very fair English.

"No rougher than we must expect," rejoined Jack crisply. The lad by now had begun to have an inkling of the situation. Evidently Bob Harding was a soldier of fortune fighting with the insurrectos against the troops of Diaz, while they themselves were supposed to be more of the same brand. Evidently they had been expected by Ramon's subterranean river, and in taking the boat they must have forestalled the real Con Divver, Jim Hickey, and Ted Rafter. Jack caught himself wondering how long it would take the latter to ride over the mountains and discover the imposture.

"We are on our way to our bivouac farther on, gentlemen," said the general, with a wave of his hand, as if to dismiss them. "Captain Harding will introduce you to your brother officers and later on I will assign you to duty."

The boys saluted once more, as did Bob Harding, and, still following the young soldier of fortune, they rode toward the rear of the column. The brown-skinned soldiers cast many glances out of their wild eyes at them as they loped back, evidently wondering at the youth of Madero's new recruits from across the border.

The boys found no opportunity to exchange conversation as they rode along. Bob Harding was far too busy introducing them to brother officers to permit of this. From remarks addressed to them, which they answered carefully in a general way, the boys soon learned that the three soldiers of fortune they were impersonating had been redoubtable warriors in several revolutionary battles in South America. Thus it came about that Jack and his chums were speedily far more prominent personalities than they cared about becoming. The officers of Madero's command they found to be mostly small planters and ranch owners, inflamed with bitterness at the freedom with which great grants of land had been made to Americans by Diaz.

Bob Harding was not backward in telling them his history, as they rode along. He had been expelled from West Point for a hazing prank, and since that time had "knocked about the world a bit," as he expressed it. He was frank in confessing that he was with Madero's command for the "fun there was in it."

"I don't see much fun in injuring American interests and practically warring on your own people," burst out Jack, before he knew what he was saying.

Harding whipped around in his saddle like a flash.

"Say, Jim Hickey," he snapped, "those are funny sentiments coming from you. You didn't feel that way during your famous campaign in Venezuela, did you?"

"Well, it wasn't so near home, you see," rather lamely explained Jack, wishing that he had bitten his tongue out before he had made such a break.

But Bob Harding fortunately was not of an analytical disposition, and he was soon rattling on again, relating to the boys, with great glee, the manner in which the insurrectos were getting all the arms they wanted by Black Ramon's underground route.

Fremont B. Deering

CHAPTER XIII

IN THE CAMP OF THE INSURRECTOS

Camp was made that night not far from the outskirts of what must have been a small town or village. Through the trees surrounding the camp the boys could catch the glint of distant lights as the sun set and darkness rushed up with the suddenness characteristic of the southern latitudes. Rumor about the camp was that there was a fair or carnival in the village. To Jack's huge delight, he found that a tent was to be provided for them, and that, if all went well, they would be able, after the camp was wrapped in sleep, to have a consultation.

But before this occurred something else happened which bore so directly on the boys' fortunes that it must be related here. Supper in the camp was over, sentries posted, and the routine of what had evidently been a long campaign taken up, when the three lads, who had been chatting with Bob Harding and trying to draw out all he knew without betraying themselves, were summoned by a ragged orderly to present themselves in General Madero's tent.

At first a dreadful fear that their deception had been discovered rushed into Jack's mind, as they arose from the ground outside Bob Harding's tent and made their way to the general's quarters. This fear, which his comrades shared with him, was speedily relieved, however. General Madero greeted them with the same grave courtesy he had shown them earlier in the day, and, after a few words, bade them be seated. Each visitor having been accommodated with a camp stool, the general turned to a written paper which he had before him on the folding camp table, and which he had apparently been poring over intently when they entered.

"I sent for you, gentlemen," he said, "in the first place, because I am sure, from what Senor Ramon told me, our new recruits are anxious to distinguish themselves, and also because I have some duty to outline to you which is peculiarly adapted for Americans to undertake.

"You know, doubtless, that the funds of the insurrectos are not as plentiful as they might be. Most of us are poor men. I myself have disposed of my estate to make the revolution against the tyrant Diaz successful." He paused and frowned at the mention of the hated name, and then continued in the same grave, even voice:

"It becomes necessary, therefore, for us to raise funds as best we may. Of course, we might live upon the country, but this I am unwilling to do. The people are friendly to us. They give us their moral support. Let us then not repay good with evil by plundering them. Rather let us pay for what we get as we go along."

Harding nodded, as did the boys. It was best to give the general the impression that they were deeply interested.

"Very well, then. But we must raise funds - and how? How better than by helping ourselves to the product of which our country has been robbed by favorites of Diaz. I refer, I need hardly say, to the American mining men who have enriched themselves at my poor countrymen's expense."

Jack could hardly repress an angry start as he saw whither this line of reasoning must lead. The gross injustice of the idea made him flush hotly, but he was far too wise to expose his hand to the wily old insurrecto leader, who was watching them with an eager look on his withered, yellow face.

"There is near here," continued the general, "a mine I have had my eyes on for a long time. It belongs to a Senor Merrill, a rancher -"

The general broke off abruptly. Jack had started so suddenly that the lamp on the table was jarred.

"Senor Hickey knows Senor Merrill?" he asked, bending his searching black eyes on the lad.

"I - no - that is, yes - I met Senor Merrill some time ago," stammered Jack. "Hearing his name again startled me. I was not aware he was in this part of the country."

Apparently the explanation satisfied the old leader, for he continued with a satisfied nod.

"This Senor Merrill is rich, I hear. But all his wealth has not prevented his miners leaving him to answer the call of the insurrecto cause. His mine, The Esmeralda, is not more than twelve miles from here. In the treasure room is stored much gold. Since we blew up the railroad, he has not been able to ship it. We must have that gold."

He paused and looked at the Americans inquiringly. Of the four, Bob Harding alone looked enthusiastic.

"It should be easy, general," he said; "if the Mexican miners have quit, all we have to do is to march in and help ourselves."

"Yes, but Senor Merrill is not unsurrounded by friends," went on the general, while Jack's heart gave a bound of gladness; "he has a German superintendent and several mine bosses. They have arms and ammunition, and it will be a difficult matter to dislodge them. Also, there are telephone wires by which he can summon aid from the regular troops."

"Well, what do you want us to do, sir?" asked Jack, with what was really, under the circumstances, a creditable simulation of disinterest.

"To undertake some scout duty. Find out just what his force is and the best quarter from which to attack the mine. And, above all, sever his communication with the outside world."

"Cut the wires?" asked Bob Harding eagerly.

"That's it. Make it impossible for us to fail."

"But, general, do not the regulars already know of your presence in this part of the country?" asked Jack.

General Madero smiled.

"The heads of bone which command them know little beyond dancing and how to flirt correctly," he said. "My flying column has, in the past two days, passed from one end of the province to the other without their being aware of it. The main part of my army is in eastern Chihuahua, blowing up bridges and otherwise diverting their attention, while I have come into, what you Americans call, Tom Tiddler's ground, where I mean to pick up all the gold and silver I can. Why not?" he demanded, with a sudden access of fury. "Is it not ours? What right have these interlopers of Americanos here? Mexico for the Mexicans and death to the robber foreigners!"

He brought his lean, shriveled hand down on the table with a thump that made the lamp shake. His Latin temperament had, for the moment, carried him away; for a flash the blaze of fanaticism shone in his eyes, only to die out as swiftly as he regained command of himself.

"When shall we depart on this duty, sir?" asked Bob Harding, after a brief pause.

"To-morrow. The hour I will inform you of later. Not a word

of this in the camp, remember. I can trust to you absolutely?"

"Absolutely," rejoined Bob Harding, with, apparently, not a single qualm of conscience.

The general's eyes were bent upon the boys who had not rejoined to his question.

"Absolutely," declared Jack, saving his conscience by adding a mental "Not."

Bob Harding, who was sharp enough in some things, was quick to detect a change in the manner of the three supposed soldiers of fortune as they left the general's tent.

"Don't much like the idea of going up against your own countrymen, eh?" he asked easily.

"No," rejoined Jack frankly, "we don't."

"Now look here, Hickey, isn't that drawing it pretty fine? Merrill and chaps like that have practically buncoed old Diaz into granting them all sorts of concessions, and -"

"I'm pretty sure Merrill never did, whatever the rest may have done," was the quiet reply.

"Eh-oh! Well, of course, it's all right to stick up for one's friends and that sort of thing, but I guess that you chaps, like myself, are down here to, line your pockets, aren't you?"

"Perhaps," was the noncommittal reply.

"Well, to be frank with you, I *am*. I'm down here just for what there is in it, and if I can see a chance to line my pockets by a quiet visit to the gold room of a mine, why, that's the mine owner's lookout, isn't it? I run my risk and ought to have some reward for it."

"That's queer reasoning, Harding."

"Say, Hickey, you're a rum sort of chap. So are your chums here, too. Not a bit what I expected you to be like. I thought you were rip-roaring sort of fellows, and you act more like a bunch of prize Sunday-school scholars."

There was a taunting note in the words that Jack was not slow to catch. Particularly was the last part of Harding's speech brought out with an insulting inflection. Jack's temper blazed up.

"See here, Harding," he snapped out, "do you know anything about dynamite?"

"Eh? What? Yes, of course. But, good gracious, what's that got to do with -"

"Everything. Dynamite doesn't say or do much till it goes off, does it?"

"What are you driving at, my dear fellow, I -"

"Just this;" Jack's eyes fairly snapped in the starlight, as he looked straight into Harding's weak, good-natured countenance; "don't monkey with high explosives. Savvy?"

Harding's eyes fell. He mumbled something. For a minute he was abashed, but he soon regained his spirits.

"Forgive me, Hickey," he exclaimed, "and you, too, Rafter and Divver. I thought you were just a bunch of kids, but now I see you are the real thing. Blown in the bottle, this side up, and all that.

"Say, do you know," he went on, lowering his voice cautiously and bending forward as if afraid the coffee-colored sentry pacing near by might overhear, "for a while I even thought you were imposters."

"No!" exclaimed Jack, starting back in well-assumed amazement.

"Fact, I assure you. Funny, wasn't it?"

"Not very funny for us had your suspicions been correct," put in Walt Phelps.

"My dear Con, I should think not. Putting your eyes out with red-hot irons would be one of the least things that old Madero would do to you. Fatherly old chap, isn't he? But, as you said, Hickey: Don't fool with dynamite!"

A few paces more brought the boys to their tent.

"Well, good night, or buenas noches, as they say in this benighted land," said Harding, as they reached it. "Better turn in and have a good sleep. And then to-morrow it's Ho! for Tom Tiddler's ground, a pickin' up gold and silver."

"And maybe bullets," came from Walt.

"Oh, my dear fellow, that's all in the life. Buenas noches!"

And Bob Harding passed on, humming gayly to himself.

The boys entered their tent and lit the lamp. It was silent as the grave outside, except for the steady tramp, tramp of the sentries. At long intervals the weird cry of some night bird came from the woods, on the edge of which they were camped, but that was all.

Jack sat down on the edge of his cot and gazed across the tent at the others.

"Well?" he said.

"Well?" came back from his two chums in danger.

Thus began a conversation which, with intervals of silence, when the sentries' heavy footsteps passed, continued into early dawn. Then, with a consciousness that the future alone could bring about a solution of their dilemma, the three tired lads tumbled into their cots to sleep the slumber of vigorous, exhausted youth.

CHAPTER XIV

"DEATH TO THE GRINGOES!"

It was broad daylight when the lads awoke. About them the life of the camp had been astir for some time, in fact. Bugles rang out cheerily and ragged troopers hastened hither and thither, with fodder or buckets of water for their mounts, for in Madero's flying squadron each man looked after his own animal, with the exception of a small force detailed to commissariat duty. From the village below, curious-eyed Mexicans began pouring into camp with the earliest dawn, and by the time the three involuntary imposters were out of their tent and had doused each other with cold water, the place presented a scene of lively activity and bustle.

"Sitting on the edge of a volcano seems to agree with us," remarked Jack, as the three sauntered off to join Bob Harding, who was standing outside his tent door, smoking a cigarette, a bad habit he had picked up from the Mexicans.

Indeed, three more manly, rugged lads would have been hard to find. Under their tanned skins the bright blood sparkled, and there was a surety in their long, swinging stride and the confident set of their shoulders that made one feel a certainty that there was a trio that would be able to take care of itself in any ordinary emergency.

Refreshed, even by the few hours slumber, and with sharp-set appetites, the boys felt altogether different persons from the three bedraggled youths who had been jounced through the tunnel, and later thrown into such a perplexing combination of circumstances.

"I feel fit for anything," Ralph confided to Jack.

"Good boy," rejoined his companion, throwing his arm about the Eastern lad's neck; "we'll come out all right. I'm confident of it."

"Unless the real Con Divver, Jim Hickey and Ted Rafter happen to show up," put in the practical Walt, with a half-grin.

"Botheration take you, Walt," exclaimed Ralph, in comic petulance; "you're the original laddie with a bucket of cold water. As we figured it out last night, we shall be far away from here on our way to the Esmeralda mine before Ramon and the real soldiers of fortune whose fame we have appropriated are anywhere near here."

"I hope so, for our sakes," muttered Walt, half to himself. Practical minded as Walt was by nature, he saw only too clearly the imminent peril in which they were moving. "Sitting on the edge of a volcano," was the way Jack had put it. He had not stated the case a bit too strongly. At any moment, for all they knew, Ramon or one of his men might arrive with the true story, and then, where would they be?

At the conference in the tent the night before, the three lads had agreed on a definite course of action. This was to get as close to the Esmeralda as they could, and then make a bold dash for Mr. Merrill and their friends. If Bob Harding chose to join them, well and good. If he did not - well, they could not force him. Somehow, both Jack and Walt had reached the conclusion that Bob, for all his vivacity and good humor and apparent courage, would prove a "rotten reed" in a moment of stress. How accurately they had gauged his character, we shall see. This plan, as our readers will agree, was a sensible one, and, moreover, had the merit of being the only way out of their dilemma. But it all hinged on one thing, namely, on their departing before Ramon or any of his followers arrived and denounced them.

Breakfast in the insurrecto camp was a peculiar meal. The officers messed together, and, of course, the boys joined them. Once or twice, Jack, looking up from his peppery stew, noticed one or another of the insurrecto officers eyeing either himself or his companions curiously.

"They think you're awful youthful looking to have done all the things credited to you," whispered Bob Harding.

After the meal was despatched, the boys expected some sort of orders to emanate from the general's tent, but apparently he was in no hurry to move forward till the errand upon which he had announced he meant to send the Americans, had been accomplished. The morning was spent by the three lads in strolling about the camp, striving their utmost to appear at their ease, but starting nervously every time an out-rider came into camp. Every hoof-beat upon the road was eloquent with signification for them. Ramon could not be far off now. In this wearing manner passed the morning hours. For some time they had seen nothing of Bob Harding, when suddenly, loud voices, in which that of their friend predominated, reached them. The sounds came from behind a thick clump of manzanita bushes, where several of the officers had been whiling away the hours at a native gambling game. Among them, we regret to say, had been Bob Harding.

As the boys, attracted by the disturbance, came up, they saw the young American on his feet in the midst of a group of native officers, who were clustered about him, angrily demanding something. From a handful of gold which the young soldier of fortune clutched, it was evident that he had been a winner, but that some dispute had arisen over his success.

Suddenly, and without the slightest warning, the young Mexican who had been the most insistent of the apparent objectors, drew his sword and rushed upon Harding, who was unarmed. He threw up his arm as the thrust came, and succeeded in deflecting it at the cost of a slash on the back of his hand.

At the same instant he ducked nimbly, and, rushing in under the swordsman's guard, he planted a blow upon the Mexican's jaw that sent him reeling backward, waving his arms round and round, like a windmill. With a howl of fury, the man's companions made a rush for Harding.

"They're going to rush him!" whispered Jack to the others.

"So I see," rejoined Walt, grimly clenching his fists.

As the charge descended on Bob Harding, he suddenly found three of his countrymen at his side.

"Thank goodness you're here," he breathed, and that was all he had time to say before the mob was upon them.

Jack had just time to deflect a sword blade, when he saw a terrific blow aimed at him with the butt of a rifle. He dodged just in time, and, as the stock went whizzing by his ear, he knocked the dealer of the blow flat on his back. In the meantime, Walt and Ralph had been giving good accounts of themselves, and Bob Harding had succeeded in disarming one of his opponents.

But they were by no means in possession of the victory yet. With howls of fury, the companions of the sprawling Mexicans charged once more, and suddenly Jack, after dealing one of them a staggering blow, saw a sword fall jangling at his feet.

Instantly he seized the weapon, and prepared to receive all comers. Now, fencing had been one of the fads at Stonefell during the past term, and Jack, under the tutelage of Mons

Dupre, the French instructor, had become an expert swordsman. With the weapon in his hand, he felt equal to facing any of the excited little yellow-faced Mexican officers. As for them, they showed an equal disposition to annihilate the Americanos.

Hardly had Jack gauged the balance of his new-found weapon, before one of his opponents, a lithe, sinewy chap, with fiercely twirled moustache, came charging in, handling his sword like a duelist. Jack parried his furious onslaught easily. The fellow checked abruptly, when he found that, instead of a green boy, he had an expert swordsman to deal with. Steadying himself, he began a systematic play for Jack's heart. This was no play duel or mock fencing match with buttoned foils. It was the real thing, and Jack knew it.

But the lad kept his head admirably. The Mexican, on the contrary, as lunge after lunge was parried, became furious.

"Carramba!" he hissed. "You dog of an Americano, I keel you!"

"If I let you," rejoined Jack, falling back a pace. The fierce thrust of his opponent fell upon thin air. The next instant Jack recovered, as if by magic, and his blade flashed and writhed thrice like a writhing serpent.

Suddenly the Mexican found his sword abruptly jerked clean out of his hand by Jack's weapon, and sent ringing over the heads of the other combatants.

"Senor, I am at your mercy!" exclaimed the Mexican, dramatically throwing his arms open for the death-thrust, which it is likely he himself would have given, had the circumstances been reversed.

"Bring me your sword," ordered Jack.

The other fetched it and handed it, hilt first, to his conqueror. Jack took it, and, placing it across his knee, snapped it clean in two.

"Save the pieces," he said, handing them to the Mexican.

"Diablo!" cried the fellow, mad at the deliberate insult, "for that you die!"

Holding a snapped section of the sword by the hilt, he drove in at Jack full tilt, only to be met by a healthy American fistic uppercut, planted with such accuracy that the Mexican's wiry form was actually lifted off its feet. He whirled round twice in the air, as if performing some sort of grotesque dance, and then fell in a heap.

"You won't bother us for a time," muttered Jack, turning to aid his companions.

While he had been engaged with his officer, the others had had their hands full.

Like a snarling pack of wolves, the Mexicans had withdrawn and suddenly made a swoop on them all at once. Defending themselves as best they could, Walt, Ralph and Bob Harding were, nevertheless, driven back against the bushes. So far as Walt and Ralph were concerned, it was a real fight, but with Bob Harding it was different. His face was a sickly yellow, and in his eyes was a light that Jack had seen before - the expression of a coward at bay.

"Keep 'em off, fellows - I'm coming!" yelled Jack, as he charged into the thick of the fray. "The reinforcement was totally unexpected by the Mexicans, and they fell back for an instant - but 'for an instant only.

"Bah, it is only another of those boys!" cried the one who seemed to be their leader, a fat, pudgy little fellow, with a thick, drooping, black moustache.

"Death to the Gringoes!" yelled his followers, their deep-lying hatred of Americans now stripped of its veneer of politeness, and lying exposed in all its ugliness.

The fat, pudgy little officer made a rush at Jack, who, instead of meeting it, ducked and caught the other by his wrist. The fellow's sword went flying, and, at the same instant, Jack made a quick turn. As he did so, the pudgy man's rotund little body was seen to rise from the ground and describe an aerial semi-circle. He came crashing to the ground with a thud, his thick neck almost driven into his shoulders by the force of the concussion.

"Now for the others!" yelled Walt; but even as he uttered the cry, there came another shout from beyond the bushes in which the battle was being waged:

"Ramon! Ramon the Black!"

CHAPTER XV

A RACE FOR LIFE

The electric thrill that passed through the lads at the words, and temporarily rendered them powerless to move, would have speedily made them an easy prey for the aggrieved Mexican officers, but that the latter were equally excited by the announcement. The mention of Ramon's name, in fact, seemed to cause a galvanic wave of activity throughout the bivouac. Men could be heard running hither and thither, and above all sounded the heavy trample of the new arrivals' horses.

In less than two minutes the last of the wounded Mexicans had picked himself up from the ground, and, clapping a hand over a rapidly swelling "goose egg," was hurrying from the scene of the sudden battle. The last to get up was the pudgy little officer whom Jack had overthrown. This fellow painfully scrambled to his feet, and, breathing the most terrible threats in his native tongue, limped off.

The boys stood alone on the card-strewn, coin-littered battle-ground. Dismay was pictured on their countenances. The crucial moment had come, and they were fairly caught in a trap from which there seemed to be no possible means of extricating themselves.

"Come on, boys," cried Bob Harding, who had quite recovered his equanimity, "here's your friend Ramon, now."

He hastened off, not even looking to see if the supposed adventurers were following him. Suddenly, while the three lads stood regarding one another, there came a high-pitched voice ringing clearly above the confusion and shouts:

"You consarned yaller coyote, you take yer leathery lunch-hooks off me, or I'll fill yer so full uv holes your ma can use you for a collander!"

"Coyote Pete!" exclaimed Jack. "Oh, boys, he's all right!"

"Oh, Jack! What are we going to do?" gasped Ralph, pale under his coat of tan, and looking about him nervously.

"We must act quickly, whatever it is," exclaimed Jack. "Thank goodness, Coyote Pete is safe. The professor must be all right, too, then. Look, there are the Mexican's horses off yonder. Let's make a dash for them, and try to sneak out while they are still looking for us."

"Do you think we can do it?" Ralph's voice was full of hesitancy.

"If we don't, we'll all be lined up with a firing squad in front of us within the next ten minutes!" exclaimed Jack. "Hark!"

They could hear shouts and angry cries, above which Ramon's voice
sounded, as if he were narrating something.

"He's telling them about us," cried Jack. "Come on; there's not a fraction of a second to lose."

Headed by Jack, the three Border Boys started on the run for the grove in which the horses had been picketed. Some of the animals were saddled and bridled, and for these they made a dash. They were not to escape without some difficulty, however, for, as they placed their feet in the stirrups, preparatory to swinging into the high-peaked saddles, a dozing trooper sprang up from a litter of opened hay-bales. He shouted something in Spanish, and made a spring for the head of the animal Jack bestrode. It was no time for half measures. The heavy quirt, with its loaded handle, hung from the horn of the saddle. With a quick movement, Jack secured it, and brought the loaded end down on the fellow's skull. He fell like a log, without uttering a sound.

"Now, forward boys!" cried Jack in a low tone, "it's a ride for life."

The others needed no urging. As rapidly as they could, consistent with making as little noise as possible, the three young horsemen rode out of the patch of woods in which the camp had been made, and emerged on the high road without being stopped. Suddenly, however, a sentry with a fixed bayonet, seemed to spring from the ground in front of them. He cried something in Spanish, to which Jack replied by driving his horse full at him. The fellow went down, and rolled over and over, as the horse's hoofs struck him. Before he recovered his feet, the Border Boys were upon the road and galloping for dear life. There was no use in caution, now. Everything depended, in fact, on putting as much distance as possible between themselves and the camp before their absence was discovered.

Fortunately, their horses were fresh, powerful animals, with long, swinging gaits. They got over the ground at a wonderful rate, and Jack's heart began to beat exultingly. Not far distant lay some hilly ground, broken with deep gullies and thickly grown with wooded patches. Could they gain it, they would have a chance of concealing themselves.

"Hullo! They've discovered we've gone!" exclaimed Jack suddenly, as behind them they could hear shots and bugle calls. "Don't spare the horses, boys; we've got to make that rough country."

The quirts fell unmercifully on the big, powerful horses, and they plunged snorting forward.

"We're kicking up dust enough to be seen ten miles," grumbled Walt.

"Can't be helped," flung back Jack, "speed is what counts now."

Before many minutes had passed, such good progress had they made that the edge of a clump of woods was reached, and they plunged rapidly into the friendly shelter.

"Where to now?" gasped Ralph.

"Right on! Right on!" shot out Jack. "Keep going till the horses drop, or they overtake us. It's our only chance."

On and on into the wood, the hunted boys rode. Their wiry horses were flagging now, but still seemed capable of more effort. Over the rough ground, though, the pace at which they urged them was a killing one. Still, as Jack had said, it was "their only chance."

All at once, from their rear, they heard shouts and bugle calls. Jack turned a shade paler. The demonstration was much too close to be pleasant. He had hardly believed that it was possible for the Mexicans to have gained upon them so rapidly.

"Guess we're up against it," muttered Walt Phelps, in his usual laconic manner.

"Not yet, by a good sight," pluckily retorted Jack. "Come on – into this gulch. It takes a turn above here, and we may find some means of getting out of their sight altogether."

Almost on their haunches, the horses were urged down the steep bank of the gully to which Jack had referred. It was about twenty feet in depth, with steep sides at the point at which they entered it, and bare. Farther on, though, it took a turn, and was covered almost to the bottom with chaparral and brush.

As Jack had said, if they could gain this portion of it, it ought to afford them an ideal hiding-place.

Rapidly they pressed forward along the rough bottom of the gulch, which was evidently a roaring water-course in times of heavy rain, but which was now as dry as a bone. It was stiflingly hot, too, but none of them noticed that. Other things far more overwhelming in importance, were upon their minds just then.

Evidently, such skilled trackers as the Mexicans, had not been at fault in locating the woods into which the boys had vanished. The yells and cries, which Jack had heard, were rapidly drawing nearer in the woods above them. But, if they could only gain the shelter of the overgrown part of the gulch, they might still be safe.

It was in this extremity that Jack bethought himself of an old trick he had heard the cow-punchers talk of at his father's ranch. They had used it in old frontier days, when the Indians were thick and hostile. The deception was a simple one. It consisted in the hunted person slipping from his horse at a suitable hiding-place and then letting the animal wander on.

The pursuers would naturally be guided by the sound of the horses' hoofs, and would follow them up, leaving the concealed victim of the chase at liberty, either to double back upon his trail, or remain where he was. His intention of putting this trick into execution Jack rapidly confided to his two companions. They rode forward through the thick brush, which they had now gained, gazing eagerly at the walls of the gulch for some cave, or other suitable place of concealment.

Suddenly Walt spied the very place which they were in search of, apparently. It was a small opening in the rocky wall of the gully, which appeared from below to penetrate quite some distance back into the earth. Its mouth was sheltered with brush and creepers, and but for the fact that a bird flew out from it as they passed, and thus attracted their attention, they might have passed it unnoticed.

A brief inspection showed that it was a small cave, about twenty feet in depth, and, as has been said, well screened from below.

"We're not likely to find a better place," announced Jack, after a hasty inspection.

"Turn the horses loose," he cried in a low, but penetrating voice, down to Walt, who had remained below with the stock.

The red-headed ranch boy slipped off the back of his steed and alighted on a rock, so as to make no tracks. He then gave the three horses, that had borne them so bravely, their liberty. At first the animals would not move, but began cropping the green stuff about them.

"Here, that won't do," breathed Jack, as the three lads crouched at the cave mouth. "Throw some rocks at them, Walt."

The boys picked up some small stones, which lay littered in front of the cave, and commenced a fusillade. It had such good results, that a few seconds later, the three horses were plunging off along the bottom of the gully as if Old Nick himself had been after them.

As their hoof-beats grew faint, Jack held up his hand to enjoin silence, although the boys had been discussing their situation in such low tones that their voices could not have traveled ten feet from the cave mouth.

"Hark!" he said.

From farther down the gully came shouts and yells, and then

the distinct rattling sound of loose shale, as several horsemen descended the steep bank into the gulch.

"They've picked up the trail," commented Walt grimly.

CHAPTER XVI

WHAT HAPPENED TO COYOTE PETE

Let us now retrace our steps to the Haunted Mesa, and ascertain how it fared with Coyote Pete and the professor, after the boys' astonishing disappearance through the balanced trap-door in the base of the hollow altar. As we know, the lads' elders were crouched at the opposite end of the former sacrificial structure, when, before their eyes, the lads were swallowed up.

For an instant - as well they might have been - the two onlookers were fairly paralyzed with amazement. The occurrence seemed to be without natural explanation. But an investigation by Pete, crawling on his hands and knees while he made it, soon revealed the nature of the device which, as we know, was nothing more nor less than a balanced trap-door of stone. An unusual weight placed upon one end of it instantly tilted it and projected whatever was on it upon the staircase below.

The professor, who recalled having read of such devices in other dwelling-places of ancient communities, was at first for following the boys into the unknown interior of the mesa, but before any move could be made in that direction, one of the newly-arrived party shoved his face over the top of the hollow altar in a spirit of investigation. He fell back with a yell, crying out that there were spirits within it, as his eyes encountered the crouching forms of its two occupants.

"What's the matter, you fool?" demanded Ramon himself, who happened to be close at hand.

"Oh, the spirits! The spirits of the hollow altar!" howled the Mexican in abject terror, his knees knocking together and his face taking on a sickly pallor.

"Hey! What's that the crazy galoot's after saying?"

The question came from a thickset man, of about middle age, upon whose upper lip bristled a fringe of reddish hair. His eyes were blue, narrow and evil, and his face was scarred in half a dozen places.

"Why, Hickey, my amigo, he says that the place is haunted," laughed Ramon.

The man addressed as Hickey turned to his two companions, one of whom was a tall, lanky chap, with straggly black hair, and bristly, unshaven chin. The other was a short, fat, rather good-natured looking little man, whose truculent chin, however, gave the lie to his incessant smile. Somehow, you felt, after a lengthy inspection of this latter, that he was by no means the amiable personage his fixed smile seemed to indicate. Small wonder, considering that his smile was fixed upon his face by reason of an old knife wound, which, in severing some facial muscles, had drawn up the corners of his mouth into a perpetual grin.

"Hullo! Here's Rafter and Con Divver!" exclaimed the bristly-moustached one. "Well, fellows, what d'ye think of this here country?"

"All right, as fur as we've gone," grunted the lanky man, "but I'm itching to git across the border and git my paws on some of that gold."

"Ye're right, Rafter," agreed the man with the perpetual smile, "that's what we're after. I ain't made a good haul since we cleaned out the safe of that asphalt company in Venezuela."

"Well, gentlemen," smiled Ramon, in his most ingratiating manner, "you will have ample opportunity shortly. I happen to know that one of the first things that General Madero intends to do is to move upon the mines of the robber Americanos, and get some of their gringo gold."

"Hooray! That's the talk," grunted Jim Hickey, who, like his mates, styled himself "soldier of fortune." But, alas! that high-sounding title in his case, as in many others, was simply a polite way of disguising his true calling, to-wit, that of an unscrupulous adventurer, whose object was to line his own pockets. A fashion has arisen of late of writing about soldiers of fortune as if they were noble, Quixotic persons. Those with whom the author has come in contact, however, have, without exception, been mercenary and cold-blooded men, to whom the name highway robber could be applied with far more justice than the higher sounding term. Such men were Jim Hickey and his two companions, who had flocked like buzzards to the border at the first word of trouble.

"Waal, thar's that greaser of yours still cuttin' up didoes," drawled Divver. "What's ther matter with ther coyote, anyhow? Say, Ramon, ain't that the main station of yer subway, yonder in ther rock pile?"

He pointed to the hollow altar, in which crouched Pete and the professor. They had heard every word of this conversation, of course, and its effect upon them may be imagined.

"That, senors, is indeed the entrance to our convenient little underground river. Ha! ha! an excellent joke on the worthy Colonel Briggs. He is guarding every point of the border but this one. Of course, he concluded, in his wise way, that nobody could cross those barren hills yonder, but, as you know, gentlemen, we go under, and not over them."

"Trust you greasers?" grinned Rafter, who was a New

Englander; "ye're as slick ez paint, and thet's a fact. But, let's see what in ther name of juniper scairt thet feller o' yourn. Seems like he's teetotel abstinence on thet altar."

"Yes, there is a superstition that the mesa is haunted," rejoined Ramon. "That is the reason why I could never get a man to ascend it without myself. If you gentlemen noticed the tracks upon the pathway, you would have seen they went only to the top of the path. Beyond that my men would in no manner go on the night we came here to reconnoiter."

"That was before you sent the order through fer the arms?" inquired Hickey.

"*Si, senor*. But now, as you see, everything bids fair to go well, and -"

"By hemlock!" broke in Rafter's sharp voice, as he drew his pistol, "thar's two cusses hidin' in ther altar."

The New Englander had separated from the others, and taken a peek over the edge of the ancient sacrificial device, to ascertain what had caused the sudden alarm of the Mexican. What he had seen had caused his amazed exclamation.

"What's that?" came the bull-throated roar of Hickey, "two men in that brick pile?"

"That's whatsoever. One on 'em is a big, long, rangy cuss, like a yearlin' colt, by gosh, and ther other's the dead spit of the school teacher at ther Four Corners, back er hum."

"We must see into this."

It was Ramon who spoke. As he did so, he advanced in his agile, cat-like way upon the altar. In his hand he held his revolver. But, as he reached the edge of the pit and raised himself to peep over, something - which something was Coyote Pete's fist - caught him full between the eyes, and sent him toppling backward into the arms of Rafter. Together the lanky New Englander and the Mexican crashed to the ground, while Pete set up a defiant yell.

"Come on!" he cried. "Any of your outfit thet's jes' pinin' fer a facial massage, hed better step this way, an' be accommodated."

Ill-advised as Pete's hasty action was, it at least created a brief spell in which he had time to leap over the edge of the altar, and, before Ramon or any of the rest could recover from their astonishment, the cow-puncher had seized the Mexican's pistol and was standing at bay, his back against the altar.

"Now, then, any gent desirous uv heving his system ventilated free of charge, will kin'ly step this way," he mocked. "Ah -" as Hickey's hand slid to his waist, "don't touch thet gun, mister, or yer friends will be sendin' you flowers."

"Waal, by Juniper!" drawled Rafter, as he gathered his spidery form together and scrambled to his feet. "You seem ter hev ther drop on us, stranger."

"Thet's what," retorted the cow-puncher, "and I mean to keep it till we can come to terms. That Mexican gent yonder knows me of old - don't you, Ramon? - and he knows thet what I say I'll do, I'll do."

"So you are spying upon me again, are you?" grated out Ramon viciously. "Not content with driving me out of the Hachetas, you must even interfere with my political activities."

"Waal, if yer gitting perlitically active with machine guns and shootin' irons, I reckon Mister Diaz ull interfere with yer 'bout as much as I will," grunted Pete, keeping the men before him covered with the Mexican's pistol. The part of this speech referring to the machine guns was a mere guess of the shrewd cow-puncher. But, as the reader knows, he had struck the nail on the head. "But see here, Ramon," he went on, dropping his tone, "we ain't here to molest you. We come out here with a scientific gent, to measure the mesa. We was going back home ter-night, an' was takin' a last look around when you come along. I'll give you my word - and you know it's good - that we don't want ter meddle with your affairs so long as they don't affect us. Run all the guns you want - for I know that's your little game - but we've got some kids with us, and it's up to me to get 'em back home safe. Let us git out of here peaceable, and no more will be said."

"Hum!" grunted the Mexican. "You forget that I owe you a little debt for some things that happened across the border some time ago. Black Ramon does not forget, nor does he forgive. I can guess who those boys are you have with you, and here is my proposal: You leave that cub, Jack Merrill, with me, and the rest of you can go, and -"

Swish!

Before Coyote Pete realized it, a raw-hide lariat circled through the air from behind, and settled about his neck. The next instant he was jerked from his feet, as Con Divver, who had crept unobserved around the altar, drew the rope tight. Ramon had seen the other creeping up, and had been talking against time till the crucial moment arrived.

Now, with a howl of triumph, he rushed at the cow-puncher, and was about to aim a terrific kick at his prostrate body, when a lanky form suddenly appeared over the edge of the altar, and fixing ten bony fingers in Ramon's inky locks, tugged till the Mexican yelled with pain.

"Well may you cry aloud for mercy, sir!" exclaimed the professor, for he it was who had suddenly come to the rescue, forgetting even the pain of his ankle in the crisis. "Even in Homer you may find it written, 'Never kick a man when he's down.'"

"*Phew!*" whistled Hickey, his smile puckering up his whole

face in an evil grimace. "This is growing interesting."

"Sanctissima Santos! Take him off! Make him let go!" yelled Ramon, dancing in agony. But the professor's long digits were entwined in his locks, and the man of science showed no disposition to let go.

"Sa-ay, yo-ou animated hop-toad, I reckin you'd better let go uv therMexican gent's draperies, er I'll be compelled ter drill yer, by hemlock."

It was Rafter who drawled out the words, and, as he spoke, he held a revolver leveled at the professor's head.

"Better drop the varmint, perfuss," directed Pete, from the ground, "they've got us hog-tied and ready fer the brand."

"By ginger! I cal-kerlate ther ain't no de-oubt uv thet," drawled Rafter, as the professor dropped his hold on Ramon's locks, and began flourishing a small geological hammer.

It would be wearisome to relate in detail all that took place at the mesa after this, but suffice it to say that Ramon's rage on the discovery that the lads had accidentally found the underground passageway was what it might have been imagined to be. As we know, a fruitless pursuit of them followed.

This over, the rascals were faced with a dilemma. The boat in which it had been arranged that Hickey, Divver and Rafter were to take passage had been appropriated by the boys.

"A thousand evils light upon them," raged Ramon, as he stood dripping on the bank of the stream. "It is a hundred to one that they also seize the three horses I had reserved for your use, gentlemen."

"Waal, I calkerlate thet sooner er later we'll cotch up ter these young catermounts, and then, by chowder, we'll mek it quite interesting fer them, whatsoever," promised Rafter significantly.

"Looks like we'll hev ter trek across ther mountains, after all," commented Hickey, no more moved by what had occurred than he ever was by anything.

But in this he reckoned without Ramon's resourcefulness. The Mexican was as clever as he was unscrupulous. Necessity being the mother of invention, he soon devised a plan to avoid the long and perilous excursion across the barren hills.

Under his direction, the wagon-bed was taken off the running-gear, and the tarpaulin cover so adjusted as to make it water-tight. Rafter was a skillful carpenter, having once done honest work in a Maine shipyard, so that the improvised boat was soon ready for transportation. Working all night, in shifts, it was ready for its voyage down the river the next morning, and just about the time our lads were eating breakfast, the desperadoes, with the professor and Pete lying tightly bound in the bottom of the clumsy craft, made a start.

The stock, including that of the ranch party, which Hickey's sharp eyes had discovered, was left in charge of some of Ramon's mestizos at the mesa. As ill-luck would have it, almost the first thing that greeted their eyes when they emerged from the tunnel was the sight of the old Mexican whom Jack had bound and set adrift. He had been rescued from his predicament by a rancher about ten miles down the stream, and had made the best of his way back at once. His prayers, apologies and explanations for the loss of the horses may be imagined as he faced Ramon's wrath. In fact, but for the intervention of Hickey, it is likely the old mestizo would have been flung into the water by his enraged employer.

A halt occurred on the river bank, while some peons were despatched for fresh horses to a ranchero known to be friendly to the insurrectos. Then began the ride to Madero's camp, which ended as we know.

CHAPTER XVII

BOB HARDING DOES "THE DECENT THING"

"Back into the cave, fellows!"

It was Jack who spoke, in a tone as low and cautious as they had adopted since the beginning of their flight.

"Say, Jack, if they ever do locate us, we're in a regular mouse-trap," exclaimed Ralph, gazing back into the cave, which had no outlet except at the front.

"Can't be helped. Needs must when a certain person drives," responded the rancher's son. "Listen, they're coming closer."

The trampling of their pursuer's horses could, in fact, now be heard quite distinctly in the gulch below. Suddenly all sound ceased.

"They've stopped to listen," whispered Jack. "I only hope they hear our horses up ahead."

Apparently the searchers did hear, for, after a brief pause, on they came again. As nearly as the boys could judge, there seemed to be several of them. They made a formidable noise, as they came crashing along below. Hardly daring to breathe, the boys crouched back into their retreat. Their nerves were strung as taut as vibrating electric wires, their hearts pounded till they shook their frames. The crucial moment was at hand.

If the insurrectos passed the cave-mouth without glancing upward and noticing it, the boys were out of the most imminent part of their peril. If, on the other hand - but none of the party concealed in the cave dared to think of that.

On came the trampling, and now it was quite near. A few moments would decide it all. Voices could be distinguished now. Among them the boys recognized the quiet tones of Madero himself.

"You say, Senor Harding," he said, using English, "that those boys came this way?"

"I am almost certain of it, general," returned the voice of the traitor. "I saw their tracks, and, as you know, called your attention to them."

"If you find them, Harding, you shall have the reward I promised. I would not have them slip through my fingers now for anything in the world. Merrill's son, you said, was one of them, Senor Ramon?"

"Yes," rejoined another of the horsemen, "and the young brat is as slippery as an eel. He and this Coyote Pete, as they call him, escaped me once before in the Grizzly Pass. I have a debt to even up with both of them."

Ramon did not mention the hidden treasure of the mission. Perhaps he had reason to fear that to do so would be to bring the anger of General Madero upon him, for he was now apparently posing as a patriot and an active insurrecto agent.

"We must have him," declared Madero, in a voice that fairly made Jack's blood run cold. Its smoothness and velvety calmness veiled a merciless ferocity.

"We will get them, never fear, general," Bob Harding's voice could be heard assuring the insurrecto leader; "if they escape now, it will mean the ruination of all our plans."

"You are right, Senor Harding," came Madero's voice; "and now, would you oblige me by seeing if that is not a cave up there on the bank of the gulch."

Important as absolute silence was, a gasp of dismay forced itself to the lads' lips. From the conversation they had overheard, it was evident Bob Harding was trying hard to cultivate favor with General Madero. In that case, he was not likely to conceal the fact that it was actually a cave Madero's sharp eyes had spied, or that the cavern held the very three youths the Mexicans were in search of.

"Let's rush out and end it all," whispered Ralph, upon whom the tension was telling cruelly.

"If you attempt any such thing, I'll knock you down," Walt assured him. The ranch boy had taken the right way to brace Ralph up. The Eastern lad bit his trembling lip, but said no more. Do not think from this that Ralph Stetson was a coward in any sense of the word. There are some natures, however, that can endure pain, or rush barehanded upon a line of guns, which yet prove unequal to the strain of awaiting a threatened calamity in silence and fortitude.

"Here, hold my horse," they heard Harding say to one of his companions, "I'll soon see if that is a cave or not."

"Bah! It is nothing but a hole in the ground," scoffed Ramon, "we are wasting time, my general."

"Not so," retorted Madero. "I mean to have those boys, if we have to turn over every stone in the valley for them."

"Ye-ew bate," drawled Rafter, who was one of the searching party, with his two companions, "I've got a word ter say, by silo, ter ther boy who used my name."

"I guess that goes for all of us," rumbled Divver's throaty bass.

Harding's footsteps could now be heard clambering up the bank. From below his companions shouted encouragement to him.

"Ef they be in thar, yew let me take fust crack at 'em, by chowder," admonished Rafter's voice from below.

"You'll all get a turn," came from Harding, in his lightest, most flippant tones.

"How can men be such ruffians?" wondered Jack to himself, as he heard. He knew now why he had instinctively mistrusted Harding from the first. Yet they had saved his life that very morning. Was Harding going to return evil for good, by betraying them to their merciless enemies? It looked so.

The former West Pointer's feet were close to the cave mouth now. Crouching back in the dark, the lads awaited what the seconds would bring forth. Jack's active brain, in the brief time he had had for revolving plans to avert the catastrophe that seemed impending, had been unable to hit upon one hitherto. Suddenly, however, he gave a sharp exclamation, and muttered to himself:

"I'll do it. It can do no harm, anyway."

"Well, is it a cave?"

The question came up from below, in Ramon's voice. The ruffian's accents fairly trembled with eagerness.

"Don't know yet - this confounded brush. What!"

Harding, who had crawled in among the chapparal, started back, as Jack's voice addressed him, coming in low, tense accents from the interior of the cave:

"Remember, Harding, we saved your life this morning - are you going to betray us now?"

"Is that you, Merrill? You see I know your name. That was a shabby trick you worked on us."

"Shabby trick! Our lives were at stake," retorted Jack.

"Hurry up thar, young feller," came from below in Rafter's voice; "by hemlock, I thought I hearn horses up ther canyon apiece."

"All right; I'll be there - just investigating," flung back Harding. "What do you want me to do, Merrill?"

"What your own conscience suggests," was the reply.

"But, if they ever found out, it would cost me my life," almost whimpered Harding, all his craven nature showing now.

"But they never will. Don't let them know we are here, and ride on. We will escape, if possible, and if we are caught, your secret is safe with us."

"You - you'll promise it?"

"On my honor."

"I'll - I'll do it, then, Merrill; but for Heaven's sake, don't betray me."

"You need not fear that," rejoined Jack, with a touch of scorn in his voice. "I have given my word."

"Say, young feller, hev yer found a gold mine up thar?" shouted Rafter.

"What is detaining you, Senor Harding," came Madero's voice.

"Nothing, sir," rejoined Harding, diving out of the bushes once more, and standing erect on the hillside; "that cave was quite deep, and it took me some time to make sure it was empty."

"Empty! By chowder, them *wuz* horses, I hearn up ther canyon, then," ejaculated the lanky Rafter.

"You found no traces of those lads there, senor?"

It was Ramon who spoke now, all his sinister character showing in his face.

"Not a trace of them," rejoined Harding, scrambling down the hill, grasping at bushes, as he half slid on his way, to steady himself.

"Well, gentlemen, they cannot be far off. We will have them ere long," General Madero assured his followers, as Bob Harding mounted once more, and they rode off, pressing forward hotly in the direction of the tramplings Rafter had heard, and which came, as my readers have guessed, from the horses the boys had turned loose.

"Say," whispered Walt, as still a-tremble with excitement the lads listened to the departing trampling of the insurrectos' horses, "that was a decent thing for Harding to do."

"The first decent thing, I imagine, that he ever did in his life," rejoined Jack.

CHAPTER XVIII

THE TABLES TURNED

How the hours after that dragged themselves on, the boys never could recollect exactly. The great danger through which they had just passed had thrown them into a sort of coma. Ralph actually slept a part of the time. An uneasy, troubled slumber, it was, frequently interrupted by outcries of alarm. Walt Phelps sat doggedly at Ralph's side, and, between them, the two came to the conclusion that, come what might, they would have to abandon the cave before long.

In the first place, the Mexicans might take it into their heads to make a second search, in view of the fact that they could not discover the boys anywhere else. In the second, there was no water or food near at hand, and if they did not take the trail pretty soon, there was grave danger of their being too exhausted to do so.

It was almost dusk when the three lads emerged from their retreat. Jack had previously made a careful reconnoiter, without, however, seeing anything to cause alarm. As quietly as they could, considering the nature of the ground, they descended the steep side of the gulch and gained the bottom without mishap.

So far, not a sign had they been able to detect of the insurrectos, and their spirits rose accordingly. Gauging their direction by the sinking sun, the fugitives struck out for the east. That, they had concluded, would be the best general direction. Toward the east, they knew, lay the railroad and the more cultivated part of the province. Westward were nothing but sterile, arid plains, without water or inhabitants, supporting no vegetation but thorny bushes and the melancholy, odorous mesquite bush.

Halting frequently, to make sure that they were not being followed or spied upon, the lads pushed steadily forward, climbing the opposite slope of the gulch, and finally emerging into a close-growing tangle of pinon and spiny brush of various kinds. Through this tangle - at sad cost to their clothes, they pushed their way - disregarding the scratches and cuts it dealt them, in their anxiety to get within striking distance of their friends, or, at any rate, of the Mexican army. From camp gossip, they knew that the regulars were devoting most of their attention to guarding the railroad line, inasmuch as the insurrectos had hitherto concentrated most of their attacks on the bridges, tracks and telegraph lines.

For half an hour or more they shoved steadily forward without exchanging more than an occasional word. It was rapidly growing dark now, and the light in the woodland was becoming gray and hazy. Suddenly, Jack, who was slightly in advance, halted abruptly, and placed his finger to his lips.

It needed no interpreter to read the sign aright.

Silence!

Tiptoeing cautiously forward behind their leader, the other two lads perceived that they had blundered upon a spot in which several horses had been left unguarded by the search parties, while they pushed their way on foot through the impenetrable brush. But it was not this fact so much that caused them to catch their breaths with gasps of amazement, as something else which suddenly became visible.

To the boys' utter dumfounding, they beheld, seated on the

Fremont B. Deering

ground, bound hand and foot with raw-hide - the professor and Coyote Pete! Both looked dismal enough, as they sat helplessly there, while three soldiers, who had been left to guard the halting-place, rolled dice on a horse-blanket.

So intent were these men on their game, that they had laid aside their arms, and their rifles lay temptingly almost within hands' reach of the three lads crouching in the brush. To make any sudden move, however, would be to attract attention, and this was the last thing they desired to do, naturally.

Suddenly, and before Jack could withdraw his eager, gazing face from its frame of brush. Coyote Pete looked up. His eyes met Jack's in a startled, incredulous stare. But the old plainsman was far too seasoned a veteran to allow his amazement to betray him into an exclamation. Nor did he apprise the professor by even so much as a look of what he had seen. The man of science was staring abstractedly before him, at the gamblers, perhaps, as he watched the rolling dice, working out a calculus or other abstruse problem. Such a mental condition, at any rate, might have been assumed, from the far-away expression of his benevolent countenance.

Without making a move, Pete rolled his eyes toward the rifles. To Jack, this motion read as plain as print:

"*Nail them.*"

This, of course, was just what the lad desired to do, but how to accomplish it without arousing the gamblers, who, despite their absorption in their game, every now and then cast a glance around, was a problem.

Suddenly Pete threw himself to the ground. Apparently, he had been seized by some terrible pain. Groaning, in what appeared to be agony, his bound figure rolled about on the earth, while his legs, which below his knees were free, kicked vigorously.

"Oh - oh - oh!" groaned Pete.

"What's the matter?" cried the gamblers, springing up in consternation at this sudden seizure.

"Oh, oh! mucho malo estomago!" howled Pete.

So well was all this simulated, that even the professor came out of his reverie and looked concerned, while the gamblers, laying down their dice for an instant, hastened to the struggling, writhing cow-puncher's side.

It was the moment to act.

Silently, almost as so many serpents, Jack and his comrades wriggled out of the brush, and, in a flash, the coveted rifles were in their possession. As Ralph seized his, however, the boy, in his eagerness, tripped and fell with a crash against some tin cooking pots.

Like a flash, the soldiers, who had been bending over Pete, wheeled about. But it was to look into the muzzles of their own rifles they did so.

Too dumfounded at the sudden turn events had taken to move, the insurrectos stood there quaking. Evidently the mestizos expected nothing better than instant death.

"Ralph, take your knife, and cut loose Pete and the professor, quick!"

Jack gave the order without averting his eyes from the three scared insurrectos.

While he and Walt kept the fellows covered, Ralph hastened to Pete's side, and in a few seconds the cow-puncher and the professor were free, although almost too stiff to move. The professor was, moreover, lame. With a groan, he sank back on a rock, unable, for the time being, to move.

Pete, however, gave himself a vigorous shake, and instantly made a dart for the saddle of one of the horses. He returned in a jiffy with two lariats, with which he proceeded to "hog-tie" the Mexicans with neatness and despatch, as he himself would have expressed it.

This done, he turned to Jack.

"Thank the Lord, you're safe, boy," he breathed, and for a minute Jack saw something bright glisten in the rugged fellow's eyes. But the next instant he was the same old Pete.

"Waal," he said, looking about him, "I reckon the next move is to stop these gents frum any vocal exercise, and then we skedaddle."

"That's the program, Pete," assented Jack, hastening to the professor's side. The old man was almost overcome.

"My boys! My boys!" he kept repeating. "I never thought to see you again."

"Nor we you, for a while, professor," said Jack hastily, while Pete, not over-gently, stuffed the Mexicans' mouths full of gags made from their own shirts.

"But, my boy, you will have to leave me again," went on the man of science dejectedly, "my ankle pains me so that I cannot move."

"But you can ride, can't you, sir?" asked Ralph.

"Yes! yes! I can do that. But where are your horses?"

"Right thar," said Pete, coming up. He waved his hand in an eloquent gesture at the animals standing at the edge of the little clearing, "take yer pick, gents. Thet little sorrel jes' about suits me."

So saying, the cow-puncher picked out a wiry, active looking little beast, and selected four others for his companions. The professor was aided into the saddle somehow, and, once up, sat clinging to the horn desperately.

"They'll never take me alive, boys," he assured them.

"That's the stuff, sir," cried Pete lustily; "you'll make a broncho-busting plainsman yet. Now, then, are we all ready?"

"All ready here," sung out Jack, who, like the others, was already in his borrowed saddle.

"All right, then. We're off, as the fellow says."

Pete dug his heels into his active little mount's sides, and the cayuse sprang forward in a way that showed Pete he was bestride of a good animal for their purposes.

Followed by the others, he plunged forward into the darkling woods, while behind them in the clearing three of the most astonished Mexicans across the border stood raging inwardly with seething fires, but outwardly voiceless and helpless as kittens. Thus, by an astonishing train of circumstances, were our adventurers once more together.

"But how in thunderation -?" began Pete, as they rode forward.

"We'll tell you some other time," broke in Jack. "The main thing now is to get away from here, for I've a notion that in no very short time it's going to be mighty unhealthy for gringoes."

"Guess you're right, lad. How're yer makin' out, perfusser?"

"Except for a pain in my ankle, I am getting along very well, thank you," was the reply.

"Say, he's all wool and a yard wide, even if he does look like a softy," declared Pete, to himself.

Threading their way through the wood, the fugitives emerged, after some hard riding, upon the bare hillside. Below them, and some distance ahead, could be seen the twinkling lights of the village Jack had noticed the night before, while on their right hands gleamed the firefly-like lights of the insurrecto camp.

"That must be ther road down thar," said Pete, pointing. "What d'ye say, ef we cut inter it below ther camp?"

"And ride into the village?" asked Ralph.

"Not to any vast extent, lad," rejoined the cow-puncher. "I'll bet Ramon and Muddy-hairo, or whatever his name is, hev thet greaser community purty well tagged with our descriptions by now. No, we'll hit ther road below the camp, and then swing off afore we hit ther village. It will beat wanderin' about on these hills, and, besides, we've got ter hev water an' food purty soon. I'm most tuckered out."

This reminded the others that they, too, were almost exhausted, and it was agreed by all that Pete's plan was a good one. By keeping to the road, they might find a hacienda or native hut where they could obtain refreshments without being asked embarrassing questions.

As they rode along, talking thus in low tones, Coyote Pete suddenly drew rein. On the dark hillside he loomed for an instant, as fixed and motionless as an equestrian statue.

"What's the trouble?" asked Ralph.

"Hush, lad. Do you hear something?"

Faintly, very faintly, out of the west came a sound full of sinister significance.

Clickety-clack! Clickety-clack! Clickety-clack!

"They're after us!" exclaimed Jack, reading the night-borne sounds aright.

CHAPTER XIX

BUCK BRADLEY'S AUTOMOBILE

How their escape had been discovered so soon, was, had there been time for it, a matter of speculation. There was little doubt, though, that some of the searchers, returning unexpectedly, had come across the bound mestizos, and had at once given the alarm.

Coyote Pete glanced about him, as if looking for some means of escape. The turn of the road that they hoped to make was still some distance ahead, but the road itself lay stretched, like a white, dusty ribbon, just before them. In the darkness, it showed clearly, and, as his eyes fell upon it, Coyote Pete's mind was made up.

"Take to the road," he cried, "there's a gulch just a little way up ahead of us."

In fact, the plainsman's watchful eye had detected, a short distance ahead, a black void in the surface of the hillside, which he guessed to be a deep arroyo.

Their horses' hoofs clattered in an unpleasantly loud manner, as they reached the hard highway, and began to hammer down it, still bearing due east. Behind them now they could hear distinctly the yells and shouts of the pursuers. They were still some distance off, however.

"Let 'em howl," remarked Coyote Pete. "The lung exercise is all they'll git. With this start, we ought to beat them out easy."

"Look! Look!" cried Ralph, suddenly pointing ahead. "What's that?"

They all saw it at the same moment - two big lights, like eyes. Seemingly, the astonishing apparition was coming toward them at a good speed. The shafts of light cast forward cut the darkness like fiery swords.

The fugitives paused, bewildered. What did this new circumstance betoken?

"What do you make her out to be, Pete?" asked Jack.

"Why, boy, if it warn't thet we're down in such a benighted part of ther country, I should say that yonder was a gasoline gig."

"An automobile!" exclaimed Walt. "It does look like one, for a fact."

"And, to my way of thinking, a naughtymobile is jes' about the ticket fer us, right now," grunted Pete. "Hark!"

There was no doubt now that the two shimmering bright lights ahead were the head lanterns of an auto. They could hear the sharp cough of her engines, as she took the hill.

"She's a powerful one, too," commented Ralph, listening. The Eastern lad knew a good deal about motor cars. His face bore an interested expression.

"I don't know who'd own one of them things down here but an American," went on Pete, as if he had been in a reverie all this time, "and if it is a Yankee, it means that maybe we are out of our difficulties."

"Well, what shall we do?" demanded Jack. "Meet it, or take to the woods?"

As he spoke, from far behind them came the sound of shots and shouts. That settled it.

"We'll take a chance, and meet them," declared Pete, riding forward.

Followed by the others, he deployed across the road, and an instant later the bright glare of the car's headlights enveloped them. From the vehicle, there came a sharp hail as the driver ground down the brakes.

"Say, you fellows, can you direct us to the camp?"

"They're nothing but a bunch of greasers," came another voice from behind the lights; "drive ahead, Jim."

"Hold on thar, Buck," hailed Coyote Pete. "I'd like ter hev a word with you."

"Say, are you chaps Americans?" demanded an astonished voice.

"Reckon so," hailed back Pete dryly, "that's what my ma said. Who air you, anyhow?"

"I am Big Buck Bradley, manager, owner and sole proprietor of Buck Bradley's Unparalleled Monst-er-ous and Unsurpassed Wild West Show and Congress of Cowboys," came back the answer. "Who are you?"

"Well, I reckon jes' at present we're in danger of being made a Wild West Show of, ourselves," drawled Pete. "But are you really Buck Bradley himself?"

"I was, at dinner-time," was the response.

"Hoorah!" yelled Pete. "It ain't possible, is it, Buck, thet you've forgot Mister Peter de Peyster?"

"What, Coyote Pete?"

"That's me!"

"Waal, you thundering old coyote, what air you doin' here?"

"Gittin' chased by a bunch of the toughest insurrectos you ever clapped eyes on, and it's up ter you ter help us out," responded Pete. He looked back, and motioned to the others, who had listened in astonishment to this dialogue. "Come on, boys, and git interduced; there ain't much time fer ettiquette."

"Yee-ow-w-w-w-w!" came a yell behind them.

"What's that?" exclaimed Buck, who, as the boys could now see, was a big, red-faced chap, clad in a linen auto-duster, combined with which his sombrero, with its beaded band, looked odd.

"Why, that's an invitation ter us ter stop," rejoined Pete.

Rapidly he explained the case, and Buck began to roar and bellow angrily, as was his wont.

"Waal, what d'yer think uv that? The derned greasers! And I was on my way ter give 'em some free tickets. We show down in the village to-night. Help you out? Surest thing you know. Turn them broncs loose, and you and yer friends pile in. Tell me ther rest as we go along."

The party of adventurers, as may be imagined, lost no time in accepting the Wild West Show man's hearty invitation, the professor being helped into the tonneau by Coyote Pete, who lifted the bony scientist as if he were nothing but a featherweight.

"Back her up, and turn around, bo," Buck ordered his chauffeur. "I'm out in my guess if we've got much time to lose."

Rapidly the car was turned, and was soon speeding in the direction they wished to go. The stolen insurrecto horses galloped off into the hills, snorting with terror, as the car began to move.

"Say, Pete, what-cher bin doin'?" began Buck, as the vehicle gathered way, "shootin' up ther town?"

"No, siree! I'm a law-abidin' citizen now," came from Pete, "and actin' as chaperony to this yer party."

"You seem ter hev chaperoned them inter a heap of trouble," observed Buck dryly, as the car gathered way.

"'Tain't all my fault. Listen," rejoined Pete, and straightaway launched into a detailed account of their adventures.

"Waal," observed Buck, at the conclusion, "you sure are the number one chop feller fer gettin' inter trouble, but you bet yer life I ain't a-goin' ter fergit ther time yer stood up with me and held off a bunch of crazy cattle-thieves, down on the Rio Grande. So, gents, give yer orders, and Buck Bradley 'ull carry 'em out."

But, alas! as the redoubtable owner of Buck Bradley's Unparalleled, etc., Wild West uttered these words, there came a sudden loud report.

Bang!

"Christopher! They're firing from ambush!" yelled Pete, jumping two feet up from his seat in the tonneau.

"Worse than that, consarn the luck!" growled Bradley, "thet rear tire's busted agin."

"Can't you run on a flat wheel?" asked Ralph anxiously.

"Not over these roads, son. We wouldn't last ten minutes. Hey you, chaffer! Get out an' fix it, willyer?"

"I'll try, sir," said the man, bringing the bumping, jolting car to a stop.

"Try, sir?" echoed Buck indignantly. "Didn't you tell me, when I hired you, thet you was a first-class, A number one chaffer?"

"Sure I did," was the indignant reply, as the driver knelt in the dust and began examining the tire carefully. "But you can't fix a puncture in a jiffy."

"This one is a-goin' ter be fixed in a jiffy," rejoined Buck ominously, "or there'll be a punctured chaffer 'round here."

As he spoke, the proprietor of the Wild West Show moved his great bulk in the forward seat, and produced a heavy-calibred revolver, that glistened in the starlight.

"Get busy!" he ordered.

"Y-y-y-y-yes, sir," stuttered the chauffeur, who had been hired in San Antonio, before the show crossed the border, and found itself in the country of the insurrectos.

"Maybe I can give him a hand - I know something about cars," volunteered Ralph.

"Then help him out, will yer son?" puffed the red-faced Buck Bradley. "It's my private opinion," he went on, in a voice intended to be confidential, but which was merely a subdued bellow, "that that chaffer of mine couldn't chaff a chafing dish."

Ralph took one of the oil headlights out of its socket, and, taking it to the back of the car, found the chauffeur scratching his head over the tire.

"What's the trouble?" asked Ralph.

"Why, you see, sir," stammered the chauffeur, "I don't just exactly know. I think it's a puncture, but -"

"Say, aren't you supposed to be a chauffeur?" inquired Ralph disgustedly.

"Waal, I run a taxicab onct," was the reply, in a low tone, however, "but that's all the chauffering I ever done. You see, I went broke in San Antone, and -"

"All right; all right," snapped Ralph impatiently. "Say, you people, you'd better get out of the car, while I tinker this up."

"Is it a bad bust-up?" puffed Buck Bradley, clambering out. "I only bought ther car a week ago, and I've spent more time under it than in it, ever since."

"It's not very bad - just a little blow-out," announced Ralph, who had been examining the wheel. "Got a jack and an emergency kit?"

"Sure!" snorted Buck Bradley. "Here, you excuse for a chaffer, git ther hospital outfit, and hurry up."

"Please, sir, I - I forgot the emergency kit," stuttered the new chauffeur.

"You forgot! Great Moses!" howled Buck. "Have you got the jack, then?"

"Yes, sir."

"Get it, please," said Ralph, pulling off one of his gloves. The boy rapidly slashed it with his pocket-knife, while the others watched him interestedly. In the meantime, the chauffeur had tremblingly "jacked up" the car.

Binding his handkerchief about the puncture, and placing the leather from his glove about that, Ralph rapidly wound some strips of raw-hide from Pete's pockets about the bandage. This done he proceeded to blow up the tire. To his great joy the extemporized "plug" held. The tire swelled and grew hard.

"It won't last long, but it may hold long enough for us," said Ralph, as he let the car down again and handed the jack to the "chaffer."

As the man took and replaced it at the back of the car, Buck Bradley regarded him with extreme disfavor. Then he turned to Ralph.

"Say, sonny," he said, "did you say you could run a car?"

"Yes."

"This one?"

"I think so."

Bradley turned to his "chaffer."

"Here, you!" he bellowed, "it's about two miles into town. Hoof it in thar an' when yer git ter camp tell Sam Stow to run ther show ter-night. I'm off on important business, tell him."

As the "chaffer" shuffled off, Buck Bradley began to hum:

"I knew at dawn, when de rooster crowed, Dere wuz gwine ter be trouble on de Gran' Trunk Ro-ad!"

"It's a good thing you got that done in jig-time, young feller," spoke Buck, as the job and his song were finished, and they scrambled back into the car, "fer here they come."

He pointed back up the starlit road.

Not more than a few hundred yards off, several mounted figures came into view. At the same moment that the occupants of the car sighted them, the pursuing insurrectos made out the automobile.

Yelling at the top of their voices, they swept down upon it.

"Let 'er out, and don't bother ter hit nuthin' but ther high places," Buck admonished Ralph, who now held the wheel.

CHAPTER XX

AT THE ESMERALDA MINE

"If only I was certain that my boy and his friends were safe, Geisler, I wouldn't feel so much anxiety."

Mr. Merrill, an anxious look on his face, paced up and down the floor of the office of the Esmeralda Mine. It was the morning of the day following the dash for safety in Buck Bradley's car, and the mine owner and his superintendent had been in anxious consultation since breakfast. In truth, they had enough to worry them. In the specie room of the mine was stored more than $20,000 worth of dust, the product of the big stamp mill.

From what they had been able to ascertain, the insurrectos were unusually active in the neighborhood. Open warning had been sent to the American mine owners, including Mr. Merrill, to be prepared to yield up generously and freely, or have their property destroyed. In addition to this worry, the mine owner and his superintendent, together with the three young "level bosses," had been practically cut off from communication with the outside world for the past twenty-four hours.

A branch of the Chihuahua Northern tapped the mine, but no train had puffed its way up the steep grade for more than three days, and it was useless to try to use the wires, as they had been put out of commission almost at the beginning of the trouble in the province.

"If I had ever dreamed the trouble would assume such serious proportions, the last thing I would have done would have been to allow the professor or his young charges to journey to the Haunted Mesa," continued the mine owner.

Geisler, a rotund German, with a wealth of flaxen hair and moustache, puffed at his china-bowled pipe before replying.

"Dese Megxicans is der teufel ven dey get started, ain'd idt?" he remarked. "For a veek, now, dere has not been a tap of vork done py der mine, und nodt a sign uv der rabblescallions uv loafers vot vos employed deere."

"That is a lesson to me in employing Mexican labor," declared Mr. Merrill emphatically. "If it isn't a saint's day carousal, it's a revolution, and if it isn't a revolution, it's a bad attack of aversion to work. I tell you, Geisler, the folks who are sympathizing with these insurrectos don't know the people or the country."

"Dot is righd," rejoined Geisler, expelling a cloud of blue smoke. "De country iss all righd, but der peoples - ach!"

He spread his hands, as if in despair. As he did so, the door of the wooden building opened, giving a glimpse of the empty, idle shaft-mouth beyond, and a young man of about twenty-two or so entered.

He was a mining student, employed as a level boss by Mr. Merrill. His employer looked up as he entered.

"Well, Markley, any news?"

"Why, sir, that arrant rascal, Pedro, just rode by. I asked him if he couldn't get the men back to work on Number Two, and he wouldn't hear of it. He says that the insurrectos are going to wipe out all the American mines, and drive the gringoes out of the country."

"Oh, they are, are they?" questioned Mr. Merrill, a grim look overspreading his face. "Just let them try it on the Esmeralda, that's all."

"You mean that you would oppose them, sir?"

"Oppose them! Holy smoke, man, you don't think I'd sit here with my hands folded and let a lot of rascally mestizos wreck my property, do you?"

"I should remarg idt not," puffed Herr Geisler.

"But, sir, there are only five of us here. How long do you suppose we could stick it out?"

"Till der lastd oldt cat be dead, py chiminy!" exploded the German. "Herr Merrill, you are all righd. Young man, are you afraidt?"

"No," protested young Markley indignantly, "but -"

"Budt what, eh? Answer me dot, blease. Budt vot?"

The belligerent German advanced till his pudgy forefinger was shaking under Markley's aristocratic nose.

"Well, they say, you know, that Madero isn't very gentle to his prisoners, especially when they happen to be gringoes."

"There, there, Markley," said Mr. Merrill, with a tinge of impatience, "don't repeat all the old gossips' tales about Madero. Why, if one believed half of them, he would be endowed with hoofs and horns, not to mention a tail with a spike on the end. If either you or Redman or Jennings wishes to leave the mine, you may. I'll write you a check for the amount I owe you now."

"Well, you see, sir," began Markley, but Geisler interrupted him furiously.

"Ach Himmel! Vot are you, a man or a Strassbourg pie? Donnervetter! Go! Raus! gedt oudt! Vamoose!"

"Sir," began Markley, turning to Mr. Merrill from this furious storm of abuse.

But his employer had taken out his check-book and fountain pen, and seemed intent upon making out the pink slips. Markley, baffled, turned with a red face toward Geisler.

"It's all right for you to talk," he said in an aggrieved tone, "but we are all young fellows. We have our careers in front of us. We want to make something of ourselves -"

"Ach!" broke out the German explosively, waving his pipe about angrily, "make deaders of yourselfs. Dot is vot you shouldt do. Go on. Dere are your pay checks. Take dem, und gedt oudt."

Glad enough to escape, Markley hastily thanked his employer, and, snatching up the pink slips, made for the door. Outside, Redman and Jennings were waiting.

"Come on," said Jennings, as Markley waved the checks, "let's get out of here. Old Madero may be along at any minute, and they say he hangs you up by the thumbs, and -"

Their voices died out, as they hurried off to pack their belongings, after which they made off for the nearest town, some ten miles away to the southeast.

"Veil," began the explosive Teuton, as their voices died away, "dere iss dree vine specimens - nodt by no means."

"You can hardly blame them for looking out for their own interests," rejoined Mr. Merrill. "It isn't everybody who, like you, would stick by his employer at the risk of his neck."

"You is more dan my employer, py chiminy, you voss mein friendt," exclaimed Geisler. "I aindt forgot it dot time dat no vun vouldt gif me a chob pecos dey dink I been vun pig vool. Vot didt you do, den? You proved yourself anudder fooll py gifing me a chob. Dink you, den, I run from dis, my dearie-o? Oh, not by a Vestphalia ham! Here I am, und here I shtay shtuck, py chiminy!"

The mine owner gave his faithful super a grateful look, and then snatched up his soft hat with a brisk movement.

"Come, Geisler," he said, "let us take a look around. Possibly, in the event of an attack, there may be one or two places that will need strengthening."

"Ach, Himmel! vot a mans," muttered the German to himself, as he followed his employer out. "I vork for him, und, py chiminy grickets, I vight for him too, alretty."

The stamp mill and main buildings of the mine, including the boiler and engine room, were surrounded by a stout fence of one-inch planking, perhaps ten feet in height. Frequent strikes and minor outbreaks among the Mexican miners had persuaded Mr. Merrill to follow the example of most of his fellow American mine owners in Mexico, and be prepared for emergencies. Facing toward the west, was a large gate in this "stockade," as it might almost be called. Surmounting this, was the bell, idle now, with which the miners were summoned to work. From the gate, which was swung open as Markley and his cronies had left it in their retreat, could be seen a huddle of small adobe houses - the homes of the laborers - and beyond these, and deeper in the valley, lay the red-tiled roofs and green gardens of Santa Marta, the nearest town.

Men could be seen moving about the laborers' huts - in fact, there was an air almost of expectant bustle about the place. Shielding his eyes, Mr. Merrill gazed down toward the little town. His keen vision had caught the glint of a firearm of some sort between the legs of a man seated outside one of the huts.

"These chaps must have advance information of some sort," he remarked to Geisler. "That fellow yonder is cleaning up a rifle."

"Looks like it voss business alretty," remarked Geisler. "Himmel, I vould gif vun dollar und ninety-eight cents, alretty, to see a troop of regulars coming up der railroad tracks."

But the tracks lay empty and shining before them, without even a freight car backed upon a siding to suggest the activity that, at this time of the week, usually reigned about the mine.

"There isn't a regiment nearer than Rosario, at last reports," rejoined Mr. Merrill, "and no way of reaching them, now that the wires are cut. If only I dared leave the place, I'd ride to Rosario, but the instant we vacated it, those yellow jackals down yonder would come swarming in."

"Dot is right," agreed Geisler, with a frown, "dey know, vorse luck, aboudt der amount of goldt vot is stored in der strong room. I bet you your life, dey iss yust votching for a chance to make idt a addack py der mine."

"That's my idea, too, Geisler, and - Hullo, who's this coming?"

CHAPTER XXI

AN ACT OF TREACHERY

He pointed inquiringly down the hillside at a young figure on horseback that was wearily climbing the declivity.

"He voss come a goot long vay, alretty," commented Geisler, taking in the dust-covered appearance of horse and rider. The gray powder, which covered both, was visible even at that distance.

"He's an American," went on Mr. Merrill, "a young man, too. I don't recollect ever having seen him before round here. Wonder what he wants?"

While he spoke, the rider came rapidly forward, and presently drew rein beside the miner and his super. He was a young man, tall, well muscled, and with a well-poised head, but his eyes were set rather too close, and there was something about that clean-shaven chin that rather made you distrust him.

"I've beaten those kids to it," he muttered to himself, as his eyes first took in the two solitary figures standing at the gate. "The rest will be easy."

Bob Harding, for it was the exiled West Pointer, could hardly help smiling, in fact, as he comprehended the simplicity of his task.

"Good morning," he said in a pleasant voice, as he rode up. "Is this the Esmeralda Mine?"

"It is," rejoined Mr. Merrill, "and I am its owner. Come in and rest yourself, won't you? You look fagged."

It was the hearty, cordial greeting of one American in a strange land to a fellow countryman. Bob Harding accepted with alacrity. He slipped from his saddle as if he were weary to death, and, indeed, his travel-stained clothes supported that idea. If the two men facing him, though, could have seen him scattering dust in liberal proportions over himself and his horse a short time before, they might not have fallen into his trap so easily. With quirt and spur, he had worked his horse into a sweat. At such tricks, Bob Harding was an adept.

But of all this, of course, neither Mr. Merrill nor his super had any idea. To their unsuspecting minds, Bob Harding was a fellow-countryman in difficulty, and they treated him accordingly.

"Phew!" remarked Harding, slipping his reins over his arm, and following Mr. Merrill within the stockade, "I had a tough time getting away from those insurrectos."

The remark had just the effect he intended it should have. Mr. Merrill regarded him with astonishment. Geisler muttered gutturally.

"The insurrectos!" exclaimed Mr. Merrill. "Are they near at hand?"

"They were," rejoined Bob Harding, secretly rejoicing to see how well his plan was working, "but they are now in retreat. The government troops met them near San Angelo, and drove them back to the west."

"I had no idea there were any government troops closer than Rosario."

"Nor had Madero's flying column, as he called it. But he found out a few hours ago. In the confusion I escaped and rode on here. I have a message for you from your son."

"My son! Good Heavens! Is Jack in the hands -"

"He was a prisoner of Madero, but he has escaped, and is now lying wounded at a spot I will guide you to."

"Himmel! Yack Merrill a prisoner, alretty!" gasped Herr Geisler.

"Not only Master Merrill, but two boy friends of his, an old gentleman, whom I should imagine was their instructor, and a cowboy."

"Yes, it must be them!" exclaimed Mr. Merrill. "But how, in the name of all that's wonderful, did they come across the border? I thought they were at the Haunted Mesa, in New Mexico."

"It is too long a story to relate to you now, senors," rejoined Bob Harding, "I may tell you, though, that they are safe at the hacienda of a friend. But your boy is seriously wounded, and must see you at once."

"Good Heavens, Geisler! This is terrible news, Mr. - Mr. -"

"Mr. Allen, of New York," put in Harding glibly.

"Terrible news that Mr. Allen of New York brings us. You were with them, Mr. Allen?"

"I was, sir. In my capacity as war correspondent for the *Planet*, I was with Madero's column. But, in the moment of defeat at the hands of the regulars, the miserable greasers turned on me as a gringo. I was compelled to flee for my life. First, however, I cut the bonds of our young friends and their comrades, and under cover of night we escaped."

Bob Harding was certainly warming to his subject as he went along. Mr. Merrill regarded him with gratitude.

"I've a horse in the stables, Mr. Allen," he said. "I'll saddle up, right away, and accompany you. How can I ever thank you for all you have done for my boy and his friends?"

"Don't mention it," said Allen glibly; "we Americans must do little things for one another, you know. But hurry, sir. Your boy was calling for you when I left."

"Poor lad!" exclaimed the deluded mine owner, hastening toward the stable. "Geisler, you must stay and look after the place. How far is it, Mr. Allen?"

"Not more than ten miles, sir," was the rejoinder.

"I can ride there and back before dark, then," declared Mr. Merrill. "If the lad is strong enough to be moved, I'll bring him with me."

All this time Geisler had been examining "Mr. Allen's" horse with a singular expression. As the miner owner vanished in the direction of the stable, he spoke:

"Dot poor horse of yours vos aboudt tuckered in, aindt it?" he inquired.

"Yes, poor brute," rejoined Bob Harding, "I rode at a furious pace."

"Und got all der dust on his chest, und none on his hind quvarters," commented the German suspiciously.

But Harding returned his gaze frankly, and wiped his brow with a great appearance of weariness.

"Is that so?" he said. "I didn't notice it. But then, I rode so hard, and -"

"Are you ready, Mr. Allen?"

It was Mr. Merrill's voice. He rode up, as he spoke, on a big chestnut, which he had saddled and bridled faster than he had ever equipped a horse before.

"All ready, sir," was the response, as Bob Harding swung himself into his saddle again.

Geisler had run into the office. Now he reappeared, holding something under his coat. He approached Mr. Merrill's side, and, while Bob Harding was leaning over examining his saddle-girth, the German slipped the object he held to his employer.

"Idt's a gun," he whispered. "Keep idt handy. Py chiminy, I dink maype you need him pefore you get through."

"With the insurrectos in retreat?" laughed Mr. Merrill. "Geisler, you are getting nervous in your old age. Come, Mr. Allen, let's be getting forward, I can hardly wait till I see my boy."

The horses plunged forward and clattered down the hillside.

Geisler watched them till a bend in the road below hid them from view. Then he turned slowly to reenter the stockade.

"Py chiminy," he muttered, emitting huge clouds of blue smoke, "I dink me dere vos a vood-pile in dot nigger, py cracious."

CHAPTER XXII

AT ROSARIO STATION

The dull gray of the dawn was illuminating the east, and the breath of the morning astir in the tree-tops, when Bill Whiting, station agent at Rosario, began to bestir himself. The station agent was not about so early on account of passengers that might be expected by an early train - for the excellent reason that there was no morning train. Since fighting had begun in Chihuahua, schedules had, to quote Bill, "gone to pot." On a sidetrack lay a locomotive, smokeless and inert, just as her crew had abandoned her. Some loaded freight cars, their contents untouched, likewise stood on the spur. That Bill Whiting, however, meant to guard the railroad's property, was evidenced by the fact that strapped to his waist was a portly revolver, while a rifle lay handy in the ticket office, in which, since the outbreak of trouble, he had watched and slept and cooked.

Bill's first task, after tumbling out of his blankets and washing his face in a tin basin standing in one corner of the office, was to tap the telegraph key. The instrument gave out a lifeless "tick-tick."

"No juice - blazes!" grunted Bill, and, being a philosophical young man, he bothered himself no more about the matter, and went about getting his breakfast.

In the midst of his preparations, however, he suddenly

straightened up and listened intently. To hear better, he even shoved aside the sizzling frying-pan from its position over one burner of his kerosene stove. What had attracted his attention was a distant sound - faint at first, but momentarily growing nearer.

"Blazes!" muttered Bill, scratching his head, and making for a rear window, which commanded a view of the long, white road. "What's that, I wonder? Sounds like a sick cow."

He gazed out of the window earnestly, and then suddenly recoiled with a startled exclamation.

"Blazes! It ain't no cow. It's an automobubble. Yes, sir, as sure as you live, it's a bubble. Whose can it be? Maybe it's old man Stetson's himself."

Chugging in a spasmodic sort of way, the car drew nearer, and the station agent now saw that there were several people in it.

"Looks like that car is spavined, or something," commented Bill. "Why, it's regularly limping; yes, sir - blazes! - it's limping, fer a fact."

Buck Bradley's auto was, in fact, at almost its "last gasp." Ralph's temporary repair had not lasted any longer than he had expected. Fortunately, at the time it gave out, the insurrectos had apparently given up the chase, and the party was not far from the hacienda of a friend of the genial Buck. At his suggestion, therefore, they diverted from their road to the mine, and swung off to this house. Here a hasty meal and a warm welcome were enjoyed, and Ralph set the car in order as best he could. Buck's friend, however, had news for them. He had heard that there was an encampment of regulars at Rosario, from which it was only a short run by rail to the branch on which the Esmeralda was located.

This information caused the party to change their plans. With the car in the condition in which it was, they doubted whether it would be possible to travel over the rough roads intervening between themselves and the mine. On the other hand, Rosario was not far off, and on a smooth, hard highway. If the information of Buck Bradley's friend was correct, and there was no reason to doubt it, the regulars were camped at Rosario guarding the line. What more easy than to explain their case to the leader of the Mexican regulars, and steal a march on the insurrectos by reaching the Esmeralda first by rail, and wiping out the band of Madero?

But, alas for human plans! The party in the auto was doomed to bitter disappointment. As they approached, and no camp was to be seen, they began to realize that their information had been inaccurate. Bill Whiting speedily clinched all doubt in the matter.

"Say, my friend," hailed Buck Bradley, as the agent emerged from his shack, "where are the soldiers?"

"You mean the greaser regulars?" was the rejoinder. "Blazes, they went off yesterday. Had a tip where Madero was, and they are after him, hot-foot, I reckon."

The boys exchanged despondent glances. Here was a fine end to their high hopes. The Esmeralda was now farther off than ever, and the auto was hopelessly crippled. One tire was worn almost to ribbons, a rim had been sprung, and two spark plugs had cracked. Every one of the party realized, as the car stopped with a sigh, that it couldn't move again until a tall lot of overhauling had been done.

"Anything I can do to help yer?" volunteered Bill, noting the woebegone faces of his countrymen.

"Nothing, son, unless you've got a wire working," sputtered Buck, who, as he did with everything, had gone into this matter, heart and soul.

"Wire!" echoed the station agent, "why, blazes, I couldn't put through a tap fer Diaz himself. The wire went dead two days ago, and I've been on my own hook since."

"What was the last word you had?" asked Jack, thinking, perhaps, that they might have some information in regard to affairs at the mine.

The agent dived into his pocket and fished out a yellow paper.

"Here it is," he exclaimed, "and it's signed by 'King Pin' Stetson himself: 'Keep freight moving at all hazards.'"

"It's signed by Mr. Stetson, you say?" exclaimed Ralph eagerly.

"Sure. He's the main boss on this road, you know, and -"

"I know, I know!" cried Ralph eagerly, "but is he here across the border?"

"Huh? Not he. He's in the best hotel in El Paso, consulting and smoking two-bit seegars. But my job's here, and here I stick."

But Ralph and Jack had not heard this speech. A light shone in the Eastern boy's eyes, the light of a great idea.

"There's a locomotive yonder, Jack," he whispered. "I can run one. I learned one summer when pop took me over the Squantock and Port Gloster line. You said there was a branch connecting with the Esmeralda. Why can't we go by rail?"

"By ginger, Ralph! Have you got the nerve?"

"Look at me."

Jack regarded his comrade an instant. There wasn't a flicker of an eyelash to show that Ralph was the least bit nervous. The experiences of the last few days had taught him much.

While Bill Whiting regarded them curiously, Jack hastily told the others of what Ralph had proposed.

"That appeals ter me as a ring-tailed roarer of a good idee," announced Buck Bradley, when he had finished.

"Waal, I'm more used ter doin' my fightin' ahorseback than from a loco, but I guess it goes here," chimed in Pete.

"An eminently sensible suggestion," was the professor's contribution. The maimed ankle of the man of science was now almost well, and, as he put it, he was "restored to his customary salubriosity."

"Then, all we've got to do, is to get permission to take the locomotive," declared Jack. He turned to Bill Whiting, who had been eyeing them curiously.

"We've got to get through to the Esmeralda mine," he said. "Our auto is broken down, and yet the fate of the mine, and perhaps the lives of its defenders, hang upon our arrival there as soon as possible. Have we your authority to run the locomotive through?"

"Say, son," drawled Bill Whiting, "put on your brakes. That's a compound, and even supposing I could let you take her, how would you run her?"

"There's a boy here who can run her all right," cried Jack impatiently. "All we need to have is your authority."

Bill Whiting shook his head.

"Sorry," he said. "I don't know you, and that loco's railroad property. I'm responsible fer it. Suppose you'd ditch her? No - blazes! - it wouldn't do at all."

"I'll give yer a hundred dollars gold fer two hours use uv that ingine," cried Buck Bradley.

"No good," declared Bill, shaking his head; "it's railroad property. I've got my job to look after, even if Chihuahua is turned inside out."

"But this is a matter of the utmost urgency," argued Jack. "Listen."

He rapidly detailed the outlines of their situation to the agent. The man was obdurate, however.

"Couldn't nobody touch that ingine but old man Stetson himself."

"How about his son?" Ralph's voice rang out clearly above the excited tones of the others.

"Waal, I reckon he could, but he ain't here."

"He isn't, eh?" demanded Ralph, hopping out of the tonneau, "well, my name happens to be Ralph Stetson."

"Oh, quit joking. You're Americans, like myself, and I'd like ter help you out, but I can't do it."

"Will you give me a chance to prove to you I'm Ralph Stetson?" asked Ralph eagerly.

"Sure; a dozen, if yer want 'em," grinned the agent, gazing at the ragged, tattered figure before him.

Ralph dived into his pocket and pulled out a bundle of letters and papers. Motioning the agent to sit beside him at the edge of the platform, he skimmed through them for the other's benefit. The group in the auto watched anxiously. A whole lot depended on Ralph's proving his identity.

"Say, blazes!" burst out the agent suddenly, "*you are* Ralph Stetson, ain't you?"

"I think those letters and papers prove it," answered the boy. "Now, do we get that loco?"

"I reckon so, if you say so. But, will you sign a paper, releasing me of responsibility?"

With what speed that paper was signed, may be imagined. In the meantime, Buck Bradley, who knew a thing or two about railroading himself, had his coat off, and was hard at work waking up the banked fires. Presently the forced draught began to roar, and black smoke to roll from the smoke-stack. By the time the auto had been wheeled in under a shed, and Bill Whiting asked to communicate with the government troops as soon as possible, all was ready for the start.

The engine was trembling under a good head of steam, white jets gushing from her safety valves.

"All ab-o-a-r-d!" yelled Pete, in the manner of a conductor, and Buck Bradley, who had stepped off after his labors to cool up a bit, began to climb back again.

"Why, are you going with us, Mr. Bradley?" demanded Jack amazedly. "What about your show?"

"Oh, Sam Stow kin look after that," was the easy rejoinder. "It won't be the first time. I've worked long enough; now I'm off for a little play."

"Won't be much play about it, I'm thinking," grunted Pete.

The engine bell clanged, a hoarse shriek came from her whistle, and the wheels began to revolve. Ralph was at the throttle, while Bill Whiting was up ahead to throw the switch.

"Good luck!" he cried, waving his hand as the locomotive swept by and rolled out upon the main line.

"Good-by!" cried the crowd of adventurers in the cab, waving their hands back at him.

Buck threw the furnace door open, and sent a big shovelful of coal skittering into the glaring interior. The cumbrous machine gave a leap forward, like a scared greyhound, as Ralph jerked the throttle open.

The Border Boys were off on what was to prove one of the most adventurous incidents of their lives.

CHAPTER XXIII

JACK MERRILL'S "SPECIAL"

The landscape swam by, the telegraph poles flashed past, as the flying locomotive gained headway. The ponderous compound jolted and swung along over the rough tracks like a ship in a stormy sea. But the thrill of adventure, the buoyant sense of facing a big enterprise, rendered the lads oblivious to everything but the track ahead.

From time to time, Buck Bradley stopped his shoveling, and, holding by a hand-rail, leaned far out from the footplate, scanning the metals that stretched out in two parallel lines ahead.

"Be like them varmints to hev blown up a bridge, or spiked a track," he muttered.

All eyes were now on the alert for the first sight of the red-brick station - the only one on the line - which Bill Whiting had told them marked the Esmeralda switch. As yet it had not come into view, but they judged it must be around a curve which lay ahead, the far side of which was hidden from them by a clump of woods. Suddenly, from this clump emerged a figure, waving a red flag. He stopped in the middle of the track, waving his flag frantically.

"Shut down!" yelled Buck. "There's danger ahead!"

"Looks more like a trick, to me," growled the wary Coyote Pete.

"Can't afford to take chances," rejoined Buck. "How do we know what's the tother side of that curve?"

"That's so," agreed Pete; "them critters might hev planted a ton of dynamite there, fer all we know."

The brakes ground down, and the panting locomotive came to a stop within a few feet of the man with the red flag. It could now be seen that he was a small, dark Mexican, wearing a high-crowned hat.

"Why, I know that fellow, he -" began Ralph. But his recognition of the fellow, whom he had seen in Madero's camp, came too late.

From the woods ahead of them, a perfect hailstorm of bullets began to spit about the engine. Fortunately, none of the occupants of her cab were struck, although the windows were splintered and the woodwork honeycombed.

"Go ahead!" roared Buck.

"What if they've torn up the track?" gasped Ralph.

"Not likely. If they had, they wouldn't be bothering to shoot at us. Let her out. Ouch!"

A bullet whizzed past the burly showman's ear, and just nicked the tip of it.

With a roar of rage, like the bellowings of an angry bull, he leaned his huge form out of the window and began pumping lead from his revolver into the woods. It is doubtful if his fire had any effect, but at that minute Ralph started the engine up again. A yell came from the Mexicans within the wood, as he did so. A hundred or more poured out, firing as they came.

"Duck, everybody!" yelled Coyote Pete, as the storm broke.

A tempest of lead rattled about the engine, but, thanks to the protection of the steel cab, not one of the crouching occupants was hurt. Almost before they realized it, they had swung around the curve, and were safe. As Buck Bradley had surmised, no attempt had been made to wreck the track beyond, the insurrectos having counted, seemingly, on stopping the dash for the Esmeralda by their ambush in the wood.

"Consarn their yellow hides," grunted Pete, "that shows they kep' closer tabs on us then we knew. I reckon they was scared to follow us to Rosario, thinking, like we did, that the regulars was there. Waal, that was a neat little surprise party, but it didn't work."

Round the curve they tore, at a hair-raising gait, but the engine stuck to the metals. Ten minutes later a cheer went up, as the red-brick station, which they knew must mark the Esmeralda switch, came in sight.

"I got the switch key from Whiting," cried Buck, as they reached the switch, "I'll throw it."

He swung himself down from the cab, and ran rapidly ahead, down the track, to the switch lever. As he bent over it, from a clump of bushes near by, there leaped a score or more of men.

"Buck! Buck!" yelled Coyote Pete.

The big fellow looked up just in time. The foremost of his attackers was upon him as he threw the switch over. Buck picked him up, and fairly pitched the little Mexican over his head. The man fell in a heap at one side of the track.

"Come ahead!" bawled Buck, while the others hesitated and held back. Ralph started the engine up, and it rolled toward the switch points. This seemed to wake the hesitating

Mexicans to life. With a yell, they made a concerted rush for Buck, but, as they did so, Ralph pulled the whistlecord, and the locomotive emitted an ear-splitting screech. The Mexicans hastily jumped aside, to avoid being run down, while Buck made a leap to exactly the opposite side of the track. As the engine puffed by, he swung on. As he did so, however, one of the yellow men made a spring for the switch. It was his evident intention to throw it, while the engine was passing over it, and ditch them.

But, before he could carry out his intention, Jack, who had seen what was about to happen, had snatched up a hunk of coal. With all his force, he aimed it at the fellow, and struck him fair and square on the head. The would-be train-wrecker toppled backward with a groan, just escaping the wheels of the engine. Before he gathered himself up and realized what had hit him, the engine was roaring and puffing its way up the grade to the Esmeralda.

"That shows us what we may expect at the mine," commented Jack. "I hope they are still all right."

"Don't worry about that, boy," comforted Buck, noting his troubled face. "The fact that Madero had his men along the line shows that he anticipated our game - like the shrewd ruffian he is. It stands to reason he couldn't have his precious squadron, or column, or whatever he calls it, in two places at once, so I guess we'll be in time yet."

"I hope so, I'm sure," breathed Jack. "If we failed now, it would be the bitterest moment of my life."

But, as they came in sight of the tall stockade and the smokeless chimneys of the Esmeralda, they saw that their apprehensions were groundless. No sign of life appeared about the mine buildings. But presently, in answer to a long blast on the whistle, a strange figure came toddling out of the gate. It was that of Geisler. As he saw the engine, with its load of friendly faces, he broke into a cheer, and ran toward the track side.

"Hoch! Hoch! Hoch!" he yelled, waving his china-bowled pipe about his head. "Diss iss der bestest thing I've seen since I had idt der Cherman measles, alretty yet."

As the brakes ground down, and with a mighty exhalation of steam and a sigh from the air-brakes, the locomotive came to a stop, Jack leaped from the cab and ran toward the German. To his astonishment, Geisler almost recoiled as he drew near, and uttered a shout.

"Donner blitzen! I voss righdt den, idt vos a trap dot dose rascals laid."

"What do you mean, Mr. Geisler? Where is my father?" gasped Jack, all in one breath.

"Himmel!" sputtered the German. "Oh, diss is an onloocky day, py chiminy. A young feller rode it to der mine, early to-day, undt told your fader dot you vos wounded, and -"

"My father went with this fellow?" demanded the boy, his eyes blazing with eagerness and anxiety.

"Ches. He thought dot idt vos all righdt, und -"

"It's a trick of Madero's to rush the mine!" exclaimed Buck, who, with the others, came up as the German was ejaculating the last words.

"Dot is vot I dink idt. Listen."

Forthwith the German launched into a detailed report of what had occurred, not omitting a full description of Harding, which was instantly recognized by the boys.

"Harding, the scoundrel!" exclaimed Jack.

"I'd like to get my hands on him for just five minutes," breathed Walt viciously.

Buck and the others, who were, of course, familiar with what had occurred to the boys with Madero's column, were also incensed.

"Such men should be hanged!" exclaimed the professor, with what was for him, a remarkable display of emotion.

"Budt come," urged the German, as he concluded his narrative, "vee hadt better be getting inside der stockade."

He pointed down toward the miners' village, where men could be seen hastening about, as if preparing to take action of some sort. What that action was, they guessed too well. Acting in concert with Madero, they meant to storm the mine, and break open the specie room.

Ralph ran the locomotive upon a switch and locked the throwing lever. Then he followed the others through the gate of the stockade. As it closed behind them, Geisler let fall a stout wooden bar into sockets prepared for it.

"I guess dot holdt dem for a viles," he said, as the bar clattered into position.

But Jack's thoughts were distracted, and his manner absorbed. His mind was fixed upon Harding's rascality, and the probable dilemma in which his father now was. Buck Bradley noticed the boy's despondent air, and sought to cheer him up.

"Brace up, Jack," he roared in his hearty way, "your pop is all right. According to my way of thinking, those greasers just lured him away from here, so that they could have easy access to the specie room. They knew that if he was on the ground, he'd blow up the whole shooting-match before he'd let them get at the gold."

"Then you don't think they have harmed him, Mr. Bradley?"

"Not they, my lad," was the reassuring rejoinder, "they wouldn't dare to injure a prominent American like your dad. Why, our troops are all massed at San Antone - for manoeuvers, the department says - but as surely as my name is Buck Bradley, the troops are there to see that the greasers don't get too fresh. You see, Jack, Uncle Sam don't want to mix in other folks' troubles. He believes in playing in his own back yard, but when any one treads on your Uncle's toes, or injures one of his citizens - then, look out for high voltage shocks."

"You have relieved my mind a whole lot, Mr. Bradley," said Jack gratefully. "I guess it's as you say. Madero and his crowd wouldn't want to run the risk of an American invasion."

"You can bet a stack of yaller chips on that, boy. But now, let's follow this Dutchman around and see what the lay of the ground is. If we've got to put up a scrap - and I guess we have - it's a long move in the right direction to have your surroundings sized up accurate. By the way, is this fellow Geisler all right?"

"My father thinks he is the most faithful and capable mining super in the country," answered Jack warmly. "I guess he is, too. I only met him once before on a former visit to the mine, but he sort of inspires me with confidence."

"Same here, Jack. I tell you the Dutch kin raise some Cain when they get going, and that fellow looks to me like one of the right brand."

Thus talking, they came up with the others. Geisler was explaining volubly his plan of defense. Buck Bradley interrupted him.

"What's the matter with boring some holes all around the stockade?" he asked. "We can fire from behind them if it's necessary, without exposing ourselves."

"Buck, that's a great idea," declared Pete, whose eyes were shining at the thought of what he termed "some action." "Got a brace and bit, Geisler?"

"Sure. Ve-e haf a whole barrel of braces and bitters," was the response, as the corpulent Teuton hastened off to get the tools.

At the part of the stockade at which they now were standing a ladder, used in some repairing job, still leaned against the high, wooden fence. Coyote Pete, struck by a sudden idea, clambered up it, and gazed over the top of the defensive barricade. As his head topped the summit, he gave a shout and rapidly ducked. At the same instant a sound, like the hum of an angry bee, buzzed above their heads.

"A bullet!" gasped Buck Bradley.

"That's wot, pod'ner," rejoined Pete, "and it's the first of a whole flock of such like. The country off to the southwest is jest alive with insurrectos!"

CHAPTER XXIV

THE ATTACK ON THE MINE

Flinging his legs over each side of the ladder, Coyote Pete slid to the ground like a boy sliding down a cellar door.

"I could catch the glint of sunlight on their rifles," he explained. "The beggars were trying to approach unseen, though, I guess, for they were sneaking round a neck of woods so as to take advantage of that arroyo that runs almost up to the mine. Better get busy with that borer."

And "get busy" they did. Holes were rapidly bored in the stockade, the apertures being of sufficient size to accommodate comfortably the muzzle of a rifle. Above each such hole another was bored, to enable the defenders to see the position of their foes. Although this work took more than an hour, there was still no sign of the enemy. But they evidently had a close watch kept on the mine, for a hat elevated on a long stick above the top of the stockade was promptly riddled with bullets.

"Jingo!" gasped Jack. "Those fellows mean business."

"What do you suppose they are going to do?" Walt asked Buck Bradley. The stout showman looked grave.

"This hanging back looks bad," he rejoined. "I guess they are waiting till dusk so as to try and catch us unprepared.

Evidently they figger they've got us where they want us, and there is no use being in a rush about finishing us up."

Buck's words were grim, but his expression was grimmer yet. The former ranch boss had been in many a tough place in his day, but revolving the situation in his mind he could not call to recollection any more dangerous circumstances than those in which he now found himself.

"Bottled and corked," was the way he expressed it to Coyote Pete, who fully shared his apprehensions.

Fortunately, behind the office of the mine, there was a small room well stocked with rifles and ammunition. This was wise precaution of Mr. Merrill's, who, knowing the Mexican character to a T, had insisted on this room being provided in case of strikes or other difficulties.

The store of arms was drawn upon freely, and each of the defenders had a spare rifle at his side. The weapons were piled by their respective holes while the besieged awaited the attack. But a hasty dinner was prepared on the coal-oil stove Of the office, and eaten and digested before there came any move on the part of Madero's men.

Through the peep-holes a casual inspection showed nothing outside but the hillside sloping away from the mine, with here and there a clump of bushes or small, scrubby trees. But every once in a while the grass would stir, or a clump of bushes would be agitated strangely, as some concealed form crept up yet closer to the stockade. Evidently, as Buck had said, the intention of Madero was to "rush" the place.

The mining village now seemed deserted, except for a few forms of women and children which could be seen flitting about. Evidently most of the men had joined the insurrectos, hoping to have a share in the loot when the time came.

"Say, Geisler!" exclaimed Buck Bradley suddenly, " got any

176   Fremont B. Deering

steam in the boiler?"

"Ches. Aboudt forty or fifty pounds. Der fires vos banked. Pud vy?"

"Oh, nothing. I've just got a little plan in my head. Now, Jack, suppose you and I take a little run to the boiler room and look about us a bit."

The boy was glad of anything to do to relieve the tension of waiting for the attack that didn't come. He gladly accompanied the self-reliant Westerner to the boiler house. They found, as Geisler had said, that in one of the boilers steam was still up.

"Now let's take a look around here, sonny," said Buck, glancing about the walls as if in search of something. "Ah! Here we are, that will do."

He pounced on a big reel of fire hose attached to the wall, as he spoke.

"Fine! Couldn't be better," he continued, as he rapidly unwound it. "Why, there must be fifty feet or more here. Now let's see. Where is the blow-off valve of this boiler?"

"This is it, isn't it?" asked Jack, indicating a valve, with wheel-controlled outlet near the base of the boiler.

"That's it. Now then for a monkey wrench and then we are all ready to give those greasers the surprise of their lives in case they try an attack upon this side of the stockade."

"What are you going -"

That was as far as Jack got in his question. As the words left his lips, there came from without the sharp sound of a shot.

Bang!

"Phew!" whistled Buck. "That's the overture. The performance is about ter begin."

In the meantime, the members of the party left at the peep-holes by Buck Bradley and Jack, had been trying their level best to obtain some inkling of which side the insurrectos meant to storm first. But, for all the sign the long, waving grass gave, or the bushes imparted, they might as well have gazed at the sky. Had they not known that the insurrectos were out there somewhere, they would have deemed the hillside barren of life.

Suddenly, however, as Coyote Pete's keen eye was sweeping the open space before the stockade, the grass quite near at hand parted, and a wiry little Mexican stepped out.

It was a good evidence of the control that Madero exercised over his men that this fellow, although he must have known he was placing his life in deadly peril, advanced to within a few feet of the stockade without a tremor.

Apparently, judging from his expression, he was astonished that no hostile demonstration came from within. But the defenders had no wish to sacrifice life needlessly, and refrained from firing upon him. Suddenly he halted, and raising his voice, cried out in Spanish:

"Will you foolish gringoes surrender and give up the gold peaceably, or must we attack the mine?"

"Did Madero tell you to ask that?" shouted Pete through his peep-hole.

"Yes; the general demanded that I should offer you this chance for your lives."

"Then tell the general, with our compliments, that if he thinks he'll get Mr. Merrill's gold without a fight, he's up against the toughest proposition he ever tackled."

"As you will, senors. Adios!"

With a wave of his hat, the Mexican ran speedily back down the hillside, and dived into some bushes. The watchers of the stockade were of the opinion that the wave of the hat was merely a bit of Latin extravagance. They soon found out, however, that it had the significance of a signal. For, as the fellow dropped into cover, the grass became alive with human forms. Coyote Pete's finger, which had been trembling upon the trigger, pressed it.

Bang!

It was the first shot of the desperate battle for the defense of the mine, and the sound that had reached the two in the boiler house.

The report was followed by a series of appalling yells from without the stockade. Mexicans seemed to spring from every clump of grass and bit of brush. It was amazing how they could have crept so close without being detected.

"We can't last five minutes!" gasped Walt, as he gazed out. The lad fired grimly into the advancing rush, however, and the others stood to their guns like veterans. Their cheeks were blanched under the tan, though, and the corners of their mouths tightened. Each one of those defenders realized the practical hopelessness of their positions.

Suddenly, amid the besiegers' onrushing forms, appeared a figure mounted upon a superb black horse. The animal curvetted and plunged as the reports of the rifles of both sides rattled away furiously, but his rider had him in perfect control.

"There's Ramon, the scoundrel!" roared Pete, gazing at the defiant figure. "I'll give him a shot for luck."

But for once the plainsman's aim was at fault. The bullet evidently did not even ruffle the former cattle rustler.

"Ledt me try!" puffed the German ferociously.

He fared no better.

"Bah! Und I thought I vos a goodt shot!" he exploded.

"It ain't that," rejoined Pete superstitiously. "The Mexicans say that Ramon bears a charmed life, and that only a silver bullet will ever lay him low."

Before the professor could make any comment Ramon was heard issuing commands in a sharp voice. He seemed to have the direction of the attack. Of Madero there was no sign, unless a small figure on a shaggy pony, far to the rear, was that of the insurrecto leader.

The result of Ramon's command was soon evident. The attackers had not been prepared for so sharp a defense, and, anxious to lose as few men as possible, Ramon had ordered them to drop once more into the grass.

This was good strategy, as it was apparently only a matter of time before the mine defenders would have to surrender, and it was little use to sacrifice lives in a mad rush against their rifles.

The attack had splintered the stockade in a score of places, but, thanks to the toughness of the seasoned wood, the bullets that had penetrated had lost most of their strength. Beyond a few scratches from flying splinters, none of the defenders were injured.

"What can they be up to?" wondered Pete, as half an hour passed and no further sign came from the besiegers.

Ramon's figure had now vanished. Perhaps he realized that the fangs of their enemies were by no means drawn, and deemed it more prudent not to take chances on the strength of his "charmed life."

And so the time passed. The sun was well on his march toward the western horizon before there came a move on the part of the enemy, and when it did come it was a startling one. Taking advantage of every bit of cover, the astute mestizos had crept around the stockade till they were in a position exactly behind the defenders. So that, in fact, for the last half hour, the alert rifles of Coyote Pete and his companions had been covering emptiness.

A yell as the attackers charged from the direction into which they had covertly worked themselves apprised the besieged of what had happened. Bitterly blaming his stupidity in not foreseeing such a move, Pete, followed by the others, darted across the stockade. As they were halfway across, however, a dozen or more heads appeared upon the undefended top.

The insurrectos had determined on a bold rush, and unmolested they had succeeded in scaling the walls on each other's shoulders.

"Good Lord!" groaned Pete, as he saw.

Despair was in the countenances of the others, but, even as they halted in dismay at what seemed certain annihilation, a strange thing happened.

With a screaming, earsplitting roar, a white cloud swept from the direction of the boiler house at the clustering forms on the top of the stockade.

It was a column of live steam that swept them from their perches, like dried leaves before a wind.

Buck Bradley's plan had worked with terrible effectiveness. Before the rush of white-vapor the insurrectos melted away in a screaming, scalded flurry. In less than two minutes after Jack had turned the steam on, not a sign of them was to be seen.

"Hooray!" yelled the boys, carried away by the sudden relief of the strain when it had seemed that all was over. "Hooray! We win!"

"Don't be premature!" admonished Buck gravely, as the column of steam was shut off. "We ain't out of ther woods yet by a long shot. How about it, Pete?"

The old plainsman tugged his sun-bleached moustache viciously.

"Why, boys," he declared emphatically, "them reptiles ain't begun ter fight yet."

CHAPTER XXV

THE LAST STAND - CONCLUSION

As the cow-puncher spoke, there came a sound from the direction of the gate which was filled with sinister significance.

Thud! Thud!

It echoed hollowly within the stockade. Buck Bradley was quick to read its meaning.

"They've got a big log or suthin, and are busting in the gate!" he cried.

A shout of dismay went up from them all. As it so happened, there had been no time to bore any holes near the gate, and the only way to delay the work of battering it down would be to clamber to the fence top and fire down into the insurrectos handling the battering ram.

But it needed no second thought to show that this would be madness. At the first appearance of a head above the stockade, they knew that half a hundred rifles from without would pour a volley at it. It would not take more than ten minutes to wipe out the whole garrison in this way.

"Nope. We'll have to think of some other plan," decided Buck. It is worthy of remark here that not one of the defenders of the mine had ever even hinted at a surrender. This was not due so much to the fact, as they knew, that it would only mean exchanging one form of death for another, as it was to their grim determination to defend the mine at whatever cost to themselves. It was the dogged American spirit that prevailed at the Alamo.

"Aha! I haf idt!" burst out Geisler suddenly, after a few minutes of deep thought. "Dere is no hope uv safing dot gate?"

"Not the least," Buck assured him. "They'll have it through in a few minutes now."

He pointed to the timbers which were already showing jagged cracks up and down their entire length.

"Veil," said the German, "der office uv der mine is made strong - oh very strong, for behindt idt is der specie room. Ve can gedt by der inside in dere and fire through der vindows. And as a last resort vee can -"

He paused.

"We can what?" demanded Jack.

"Nefer mindt. I dell you later. Now is dot agreed upon?"

"It's about all we can do, I guess," grunted Pete, "unless we stay here to be shot down."

"Den come mit me."

The German rapidly led the way across the yard to the office building. As he closed and barred the door, they noted that it was lined inside with steel, strongly riveted to the oak. The windows also had steel shutters, cleverly concealed, in cases into which they slid, from casual view. In the windows, as well as in the door, were small apertures for firing through.

"Why, it's a regular fort!" exclaimed Ralph, as the shutters clanged to with a harsh, grating sound.

"You bet my life idt's a fort," agreed Herr Geisler, "undt ledt me tell you dot you needt a fort ven you have a specie room by dis country."

"Then the specie room is near us?"

"In there."

The German pointed over his shoulder at a door in the rear of the office.

"Idt is steel walled, undt dere is a combination lock on der door. Even if dey should kill us all, dey still have a tough nut to crack."

The German spoke calmly, and his blond features were absolutely unruffled. No emotion appeared either on the weathered countenances of Coyote Pete or Buck Bradley. The professor's face, though, was ashen, but he uttered never a word. As for the boys, who shall blame them if it is said that their hearts were beating wildly, their mouths felt dry, and their brains throbbed.

It was the last stand, and they all realized it.

Unless help should come from an unforeseen source, they were bound to perish miserably at the hands of the insurrectos.

Suddenly, there was a great crashing, rending sound from without. Instantly a chorus of wild yells arose on the air, and shots were fired as if in exultation.

"They've busted the gate!" exclaimed Buck.

Peering through the apertures in the door and windows, they could see the hoard come pouring into the yard of the mine. At first they came cautiously. They evidently recollected the steam, and feared another ambush. In a few minutes, however, their confidence returned. The watchers could see a little man dart out from among the crowd and point toward the specie room and the office structure.

"The gold is within, my brothers!" he shouted in Spanish.

"Bodderation tage dot feller," sputtered Geisler, "a veek ago he vos der best vorkman ve hadt by der mine, undt now look at him."

With a howl, the insurrectos charged on the hut. The lust of gold was in their veins, and they minded the volley poured into them by the defenders no more than if it had been so much rain. Several of them fell, but it seemed to make no difference to the others. They charged right up to the very doors of the place. Some of them even tore at the walls as if they imagined they could demolish them and get at the gringo gold.

"Dot is vot goldt does for mens," philosophically remarked the German, as he gazed at the onrush, firing methodically at the same time.

Jack, Ralph, and Walt were at one of the windows, while the professor and Coyote Pete defended the other. During the mad rush for the office, they all did considerable execution, without, of course, any cost to themselves. The Mexicans, to be sure, returned the fire furiously, but their bullets "pinged" harmlessly against the steel shutters, or buried themselves in the thick, wooden walls.

Suddenly there came an angry shout from some one evidently in authority among the insurrectos. Instantly the attack melted away, the retreating men dragging their wounded with them. It was Jack's first sight of real warfare, and it made his blood, as well as that of the others, run cold.

"Now what are they up to?" wondered Buck, as this sudden

cessation of activities came.

"Search me," rejoined Coyote Pete, "but it's some deviltry, you can bet on that - that voice was Ramon's. He's got a plan in his head to get us out of here."

"Well, he'll have a man's-sized job on his hands," rejoined Buck, calmly reloading the magazine of his rifle and running a cleaning rod through the foul barrel.

The others employed their time in the same manner. Thus they waited for what seemed an interminable age. Still there was no sign of the Mexicans. The yard without was empty of life.

"If they don't show up in a few minutes, what say if we open the door and make a rush for it?" asked Jack.

"As good an idea as any," rejoined Buck, "but what I would like to know right now is what they can be doing."

"Queer, ain't it?" said Pete.

They all agreed that it was, but not one could hit upon an explanation that seemed plausible.

Suddenly, Buck, who had been sniffing suspiciously for a few seconds, gave a sharp exclamation.

"Do you fellows smell anything?"

"No -" began Jack, and then:

"Good heavens, yes! Something's on fire!"

"That's right," agreed Pete, without a quaver in his voice. "The varmints hev set fire to the building from the rear."

"That's what!" rejoined Buck, "and we can't get within a mile of them. I don't suppose there are any rifle holes in the specie room are there, Mr. Geisler?"

"Nodt a vun," rejoined the German, in a peculiar voice, and then they noticed, in the gloomy light of the closed-up place, that his face was ashen white.

It was clear that the German was badly frightened. His knees seemed to be knocking together, in fact. Small wonder, too. The sharp, acrid smell of blazing wood was in the air now. They could hear the crackle of the flames as they devoured the wooden outer walls of the specie room.

"Come, cheer up, my man," Buck admonished the quaking German. "Why you've stood it all through like a major, and -"

"Idt ain't dot. Idt ain't dose mis-er-able creasers dot I'm afraid of," rejoined the German in a quavering voice.

"What then?"

"Dot room behindt us contains, besides der specie, almost a ton of dynamite!"

"Great jumping wildcats!"

The exclamation dropped from Buck's lips. The others were too thunderstruck to utter a word.

"There's only one thing to do," spoke up Pete, his words fairly tumbling out of his mouth in his haste. "We must open the door and, at a signal, make a rush for it. We may never get through, but it's better than being blown up as we shall be if we remain here. The insurrectos must have left their horses somewhere near at hand. Maybe we can find them and escape."

"It's one chance in a thousand!" exclaimed Jack. "But perhaps this will be the thousandth time."

"Let us pray so!" exclaimed the professor fervently.

Buck had sprung to the door. His hand was on the bar. He knew, as did they all, that there was not an instant to lose. Their lives hung by a hair. At any moment the flames might reach the dynamite and then - annihilation, swift and terrible.

"Now!" he cried, dropping the bar. A strange light, not of fear but of determination, gleamed in his eyes.

Clang!

The bar fell to the ground, and the besieged party dashed forth, firing as they emerged.

Suddenly, from without, and just as the insurrectos espied the daring sortie, there came the shrill notes of a bugle. At the same instant a ringing cheer came over the top of the stockade.

What could it all mean? As if in a dream, the boys saw the insurrectos picking up their rifles and rushing toward the gate. But before they could reach it, a glorious sight greeted them.

A regiment of regular Mexican cavalry, the men with their carbines unslung, pouring a disastrous hail into the swarming insurrectos, suddenly swung through the shattered gateway.

Shouts and cries responded everywhere within the stockade. The terrified insurrectos dropped their rifles and ran hither and thither in mad, frenzied panic. It was every one for himself. Over the stockade they clambered, many paying toll with their lives before the carbines of Diaz's troopers.

But in the midst of the turmoil a clear, boyish voice arose.

"Back! Get back, for heaven's sake!"

The officer of the Mexican regulars heard, and wheeled his

men. He recognized the thrill of warning in Jack Merrill's tones.

Stumbling forward, the suddenly relieved party of Americans darted toward the gate for their lives. On down the hillside they fled, with the cavalry surging behind and about them.

"What is it? What is the matter?" gasped the officer in English, as Jack stumbled along at his side.

The lad gasped out one word:

"Dynamite!"

Hardly had it fallen from his lips before the ground shook as if convulsed with an earthquake. A red flame shot skyward behind them, and a mighty, reverberating roar went rumbling and echoing over the countryside.

The flames had reached the explosive.

Almost at the same instant a shower of embers, debris, and odds and ends of all descriptions came showering about the retreating force. Several were cut and bruised by the shower, but none seriously.

Fortunately, also, beyond causing several of the cavalry horses to bolt in mad terror, no damage was done to the troops or our friends. The situation was rapidly explained to the wondering officer whose name was Captain Dominguez, in command of the force detailed to guard the railroad.

"We learned at Rosario that you had come to the mine," he said, in explanation of the troops' opportune arrival, "and, knowing that Madero was in the habit of raiding mines and was in the neighborhood, we made top speed to the rescue."

"And we're all mighty happy to meet you, you kin bet, captain," chimed in Buck, "but ef yer hadn't arrived when you did, we would not have had the pleasure."

"No, I can see that," rejoined the young officer, gazing off down the hillside.

In every direction could be seen Mexican troopers pursuing rebels, shooting them down, without mercy when fight was shown, in other cases, making prisoners. The rout of the insurrectos was complete and final.

Suddenly a figure on horseback was seen coming at a hard gallop toward the little group surrounding Captain Dominguez.

"It's Harding!" gasped Jack, as the figure drew closer, and indeed it was the former West Pointer. But he was in sad case. His shirt was torn almost from his back, his features blackened and seared, and a red stain showed upon his chest.

"He was in that explosion, the precious scoundrel!" grated out Buck, as his eye took in these details. "He was one of the fellers that set that fire."

Straight for the little party Harding rode. But before he reached them two Mexican troopers interposed. They raised their carbines and the next moment would have been Harding's last, but for Jack.

"Don't let them fire!" he begged.

The captain shouted an order and the troopers lowered their weapons. Straight on for the party rode Harding, toppling out of his saddle as he reached them. The fellow was badly wounded. He had been struck by a flying splinter in the explosion of the dynamite.

"Ah, a countryman of yours," remarked the captain, with a tinge of sarcasm. "You should be proud of him, senors."

But Jack was on his knees beside Harding.

"Where is my father, Harding? Tell me quick!"

"I will," gasped out the wounded man. "Madero had him tied in that grove yonder. He wished him to see the destruction of his mine, he said, and -"

The man fainted. Rascal as they knew him to be, the boys were soon applying such remedies as they could - all but Jack, that is. The boy, on Harding's pony, was off at lightning speed for the grove Harding had indicated. As he entered it, he spied Mr. Merrill tied, as Harding had said, to a tree. Of the meeting between father and son we prefer to let each reader draw his own mental picture.

"Merrill, forgive me!" breathed Harding, who had recovered from his swoon a few moments after as Jack and his father came up from the grove.

"I may forgive you, Harding," rejoined Jack, "but I can never forget."

And forgive Jack did, as he showed by interceding for the man and having him removed to a hospital near Rosario. Harding ultimately recovered and of his further movements we have no knowledge. He fared better, however, than Hickey, Divver and Rafter, who were captured by the government forces and sentenced to death by a summary court-martial.

Mr. Merrill rapidly explained that he had ridden ten miles or more from the mine with Harding before he became suspicious. He then asked Harding point blank where his son was, and the fellow's reply had been to give a peculiar whistle. Thereupon several insurrectos had leaped from the bushes and made the mine owner captive. As Harding had told Jack, Madero, with fiendish cruelty, had tied him in the grove to witness the annihilation of his own mine.

After a short pause, during which restoratives were administered to the almost exhausted Americans from the Mexican officers' field kit, they headed for the mine to ascertain what damage had been done by the explosion. Almost the first object that met their eyes as they neared the stockade was a jagged break in the structure caused by a large object that had come crashing down upon it. On closer view this proved to be the steel safe in which the gold had been placed. On opening the receptacle, everything was found intact, a fact which the makers of the safe are now using as a testimonial, as you may have noticed as you passed their Broadway store. The testimonial is signed by Conrad Geisler, who is now Mr. Merrill's partner.

Well, there is not much more to tell of this part of the Border Boys' adventures. As it may be of interest, however, to relate the further history of the underground river and the Haunted Mesa, we shall set it down here. Ramon escaped from the general disaster to the insurrectos at the Esmeralda Mine, and apparently rode straight from there to the mouth of the underground river he had long used to such good advantage. At any rate, when the boys visited it later, they found that a cunningly set explosion had completely blocked the passage for navigation, and the secret route of the forgotten race was forever closed to man. As for the Mesa, you can read all about it scientifically described in Professor Wintergreen's monograph on the subject.

The ponies and the redoubtable One Spot, Two Spot, and Three Spot were located at the Mesa, where they had been left in charge of Ramon's men. All were fat and in good condition, and Firewater was very glad to see his young master again.

By the way, Bill Whiting is now stationed in charge at the important railroad center of El Paso.

* * * * * *

"Wall," remarked Pete, as they rode toward the ranch one

evening, "I guess things 'ull be quiet now fer a while."

"Hope so," rejoined Buck Bradley. "I wired Stow ter bring my show ter Maguez and you can all have free passes."

Jack thanked the genial showman on behalf of his companions, and then reminded him that Ramon was still at large, although the insurrectos were almost subjugated.

"Yes, consarn that pesky critter with the finest horse I ever set eyes on, - and while he's alive ther'll be no peace along the border."

"That's right," agreed Pete. "He's a natural born trouble-maker. But I guess so far as we are concerned we are through with him."

But Coyote Pete, accurate as were his usual judgments, was wrong in this. Black Ramon and his horse will figure again in these stories, and it will then be seen how the boys finally brought him to book for his misdeeds.

* * * * * *

The shadows are falling over the plains and the foothills are purpling in the clear twilight of the southwest. In the sunset sky the bright lone star of evening glimmers. Let us now say good night and good luck to the Border Boys till we meet them again in a new volume of their adventures to be called: "THE BORDER BOYS WITH THE MEXICAN RANGERS."

Fremont B. Deering

Choose from Thousands of 1stWorldLibrary Classics By

A. M. Barnard	C. M. Ingleby	Elizabeth Gaskell
Ada Leverson	Carolyn Wells	Elizabeth McCracken
Adolphus William Ward	Catherine Parr Traill	Elizabeth Von Arnim
Aesop	Charles A. Eastman	Ellem Key
Agatha Christie	Charles Amory Beach	Emerson Hough
Alexander Aaronsohn	Charles Dickens	Emilie F. Carlen
Alexander Kielland	Charles Dudley Warner	Emily Dickinson
Alexandre Dumas	Charles Farrar Browne	Enid Bagnold
Alfred Gatty	Charles Ives	Enilor Macartney Lane
Alfred Ollivant	Charles Kingsley	Erasmus W. Jones
Alice Duer Miller	Charles Klein	Ernie Howard Pie
Alice Turner Curtis	Charles Hanson Towne	Ethel May Dell
Alice Dunbar	Charles Lathrop Pack	Ethel Turner
Allen Chapman	Charles Romyn Dake	Ethel Watts Mumford
Ambrose Bierce	Charles Whibley	Eugenie Foa
Amelia E. Barr	Charles Willing Beale	Eugene Wood
Amory H. Bradford	Charlotte M. Braeme	Eustace Hale Ball
Andrew Lang	Charlotte M. Yonge	Evelyn Everett-green
Andrew McFarland Davis	Charlotte Perkins Stetson	Everard Cotes
Andy Adams	Clair W. Hayes	F. H. Cheley
Anna Alice Chapin	Clarence Day Jr.	F. J. Cross
Anna Sewell	Clarence E. Mulford	F. Marion Crawford
Annie Besant	Clemence Housman	Federick Austin Ogg
Annie Hamilton Donnell	Confucius	Ferdinand Ossendowski
Annie Payson Call	Coningsby Dawson	Francis Bacon
Annie Roe Carr	Cornelis DeWitt Wilcox	Francis Darwin
Annonaymous	Cyril Burleigh	Frances Hodgson Burnett
Anton Chekhov	D. H. Lawrence	Frances Parkinson Keyes
Arnold Bennett	Daniel Defoe	Frank Gee Patchin
Arthur Conan Doyle	David Garnett	Frank Harris
Arthur M. Winfield	Dinah Craik	Frank Jewett Mather
Arthur Ransome	Don Carlos Janes	Frank L. Packard
Arthur Schnitzler	Donald Keyhoe	Frank V. Webster
Atticus	Dorothy Kilner	Frederic Stewart Isham
B.H. Baden-Powell	Dougan Clark	Frederick Trevor Hill
B. M. Bower	Douglas Fairbanks	Frederick Winslow Taylor
B. C. Chatterjee	E. Nesbit	Friedrich Kerst
Baroness Emmuska Orczy	E.P.Roe	Friedrich Nietzsche
Baroness Orczy	E. Phillips Oppenheim	Fyodor Dostoyevsky
Basil King	Earl Barnes	G.A. Henty
Bayard Taylor	Edgar Rice Burroughs	G.K. Chesterton
Ben Macomber	Edith Van Dyne	Gabrielle E. Jackson
Bertha Muzzy Bower	Edith Wharton	Garrett P. Serviss
Bjornstjerne Bjornson	Edward Everett Hale	Gaston Leroux
Booth Tarkington	Edward J. O'Biren	George A. Warren
Boyd Cable	Edward S. Ellis	George Ade
Bram Stoker	Edwin L. Arnold	Geroge Bernard Shaw
C. Collodi	Eleanor Atkins	George Durston
C. E. Orr	Eliot Gregory	George Ebers

George Eliot
George Gissing
George MacDonald
George Meredith
George Orwell
George Sylvester Viereck
George Tucker
George W. Cable
George Wharton James
Gertrude Atherton
Gordon Casserly
Grace E. King
Grace Gallatin
Grace Greenwood
Grant Allen
Guillermo A. Sherwell
Gulielma Zollinger
Gustav Flaubert
H. A. Cody
H. B. Irving
H.C. Bailey
H. G. Wells
H. H. Munro
H. Irving Hancock
H. Rider Haggard
H. W. C. Davis
Haldeman Julius
Hall Caine
Hamilton Wright Mabie
Hans Christian Andersen
Harold Avery
Harold McGrath
Harriet Beecher Stowe
Harry Castlemon
Harry Coghill
Harry Houidini
Hayden Carruth
Helent Hunt Jackson
Helen Nicolay
Hendrik Conscience
Hendy David Thoreau
Henri Barbusse
Henrik Ibsen
Henry Adams
Henry Ford
Henry Frost
Henry James
Henry Jones Ford
Henry Seton Merriman
Henry W Longfellow
Herbert A. Giles

Herbert Carter
Herbert N. Casson
Herman Hesse
Hildegard G. Frey
Homer
Honore De Balzac
Horace B. Day
Horace Walpole
Horatio Alger Jr.
Howard Pyle
Howard R. Garis
Hugh Lofting
Hugh Walpole
Humphry Ward
Ian Maclaren
Inez Haynes Gillmore
Irving Bacheller
Isabel Hornibrook
Israel Abrahams
Ivan Turgenev
J.G.Austin
J. Henri Fabre
J. M. Barrie
J. Macdonald Oxley
J. S. Fletcher
J. S. Knowles
J. Storer Clouston
Jack London
Jacob Abbott
James Allen
James Andrews
James Baldwin
James Branch Cabell
James DeMille
James Joyce
James Lane Allen
James Lane Allen
James Oliver Curwood
James Oppenheim
James Otis
James R. Driscoll
Jane Austen
Jane L. Stewart
Janet Aldridge
Jens Peter Jacobsen
Jerome K. Jerome
John Burroughs
John Cournos
John F. Kennedy
John Gay
John Glasworthy

John Habberton
John Joy Bell
John Kendrick Bangs
John Milton
John Philip Sousa
Jonas Lauritz Idemil Lie
Jonathan Swift
Joseph A. Altsheler
Joseph Carey
Joseph Conrad
Joseph E. Badger Jr
Joseph Hergesheimer
Joseph Jacobs
Jules Vernes
Julian Hawthrone
Julie A Lippmann
Justin Huntly McCarthy
Kakuzo Okakura
Kenneth Grahame
Kenneth McGaffey
Kate Langley Bosher
Kate Langley Bosher
Katherine Cecil Thurston
Katherine Stokes
L. A. Abbot
L. T. Meade
L. Frank Baum
Latta Griswold
Laura Dent Crane
Laura Lee Hope
Laurence Housman
Lawrence Beasley
Leo Tolstoy
Leonid Andreyev
Lewis Carroll
Lewis Sperry Chafer
Lilian Bell
Lloyd Osbourne
Louis Hughes
Louis Tracy
Louisa May Alcott
Lucy Fitch Perkins
Lucy Maud Montgomery
Luther Benson
Lydia Miller Middleton
Lyndon Orr
M. Corvus
M. H. Adams
Margaret E. Sangster
Margret Howth
Margaret Vandercook

Margret Penrose
Maria Edgeworth
Maria Thompson Daviess
Mariano Azuela
Marion Polk Angellotti
Mark Overton
Mark Twain
Mary Austin
Mary Catherine Crowley
Mary Cole
Mary Hastings Bradley
Mary Roberts Rinehart
Mary Rowlandson
M. Wollstonecraft Shelley
Maud Lindsay
Max Beerbohm
Myra Kelly
Nathaniel Hawthrone
Nicolo Machiavelli
O. F. Walton
Oscar Wilde
Owen Johnson
P.G. Wodehouse
Paul and Mabel Thorne
Paul G. Tomlinson
Paul Severing
Percy Brebner
Peter B. Kyne
Plato
R. Derby Holmes
R. L. Stevenson
R. S. Ball
Rabindranath Tagore
Rahul Alvares
Ralph Bonehill
Ralph Henry Barbour
Ralph Victor
Ralph Waldo Emmerson
Rene Descartes
Rex Beach

Rex E. Beach
Richard Harding Davis
Richard Jefferies
Richard Le Gallienne
Robert Barr
Robert Frost
Robert Gordon Anderson
Robert L. Drake
Robert Lansing
Robert Lynd
Robert Michael Ballantyne
Robert W. Chambers
Rosa Nouchette Carey
Rudyard Kipling
Samuel B. Allison
Samuel Hopkins Adams
Sarah Bernhardt
Sarah C. Hallowell
Selma Lagerlof
Sherwood Anderson
Sigmund Freud
Standish O'Grady
Stanley Weyman
Stella Benson
Stella M. Francis
Stephen Crane
Stewart Edward White
Stijn Streuvels
Swami Abhedananda
Swami Parmananda
T. S. Ackland
T. S. Arthur
The Princess Der Ling
Thomas A. Janvier
Thomas A Kempis
Thomas Anderton
Thomas Bailey Aldrich
Thomas Bulfinch
Thomas De Quincey
Thomas Dixon

Thomas H. Huxley
Thomas Hardy
Thomas More
Thornton W. Burgess
U. S. Grant
Valentine Williams
Various Authors
Vaughan Kester
Victor Appleton
Victoria Cross
Virginia Woolf
Wadsworth Camp
Walter Camp
Walter Scott
Washington Irving
Wilbur Lawton
Wilkie Collins
Willa Cather
Willard F. Baker
William Dean Howells
William le Queux
W. Makepeace Thackeray
William W. Walter
William Shakespeare
Winston Churchill
Yei Theodora Ozaki
Yogi Ramacharaka
Young E. Allison
Zane Grey